ISRAEL, YESTERDAY AND TODAY

Published by

CROSSWAYS INTERNATIONAL, INC
7930 Computer Ave S
Minneapolis, MN 55435
1-800-257-7308
www.crossways.org

All rights reserved. No part of this publication may be reproduced, stored in a retrieval system, or transmitted in any form or by any means, electronic, mechanical, photocopying, recording or otherwise, without the prior permission of the copyright owners.

Seven writers have contributed to this publication:

Erich Renner, former lecturer in Old Testament at Luther Seminary, North Adelaide, South Australia.

Dewey M. Beegle, former lecturer in Old Testament at Wesley Theological Seminary, Washington, D.C.

Michael Prior, C.M., professor of Biblical Studies at the University of Surrey, England, and visiting professor in Bethlehem University, Palestine. He is a biblical scholar, Chair of the Catholic Biblical Association of Great Britain, and author of *Zionism and the State of Israel: A Moral Inquiry*, and *The Bible and Colonialism: A Moral Critique*.

John Mahoney, Executive Director of New York-based *Americans for Middle East Understanding*. He has a Doctor of Sacred Theology Degree from the Gregorian University in Rome, and has taught religious studies at three colleges and universities in or near Boston MA, and at Franklin College, Lugano, Switzerland.

Jimmy Carter, Former President of the United States.

Kenneth E. Bailey, Presbyterian scholar whose areas of speciality are the cultural background and literary forms of the New Testament. He has written extensively in English and Arabic, taught for forty years in the Middle East, and lectured in many countries; venues include Cambridge and Oxford Universities. He is also Canon Theologian of an Episcopal diocese.

Harry Wendt, President of Crossways International, Minneapolis, MN. He has developed numerous Bible study programs which have been translated into 35 languages and are being used in about 45 countries. He has conducted seminars in 32 countries.

CROSSWAYS INTERNATIONAL INC. expresses its thanks to:

The directors of Lutheran Publishing House, Adelaide, South Australia for permission to reprint *Israel, Yesterday and Today*, by Erich Renner, © 1978.

David Noel Freedman, Director of Pryor Pettengill, publisher, Ann Arbor, Michigan, for permission to reprint *Modern Israel: Past and Future*. This work is a chapter from Dewey M. Beegle's larger work entitled, *Prophecy and Prediction*, Pryor Pettengill, publisher, © 1978.

John F. Mahoney, Executive Director of Americans for Middle East Understanding, for permission to reprint two articles which appeared in *The Link*, the official publication of AMEU. The articles are: *Confronting the Bible's Ethnic Cleansing in Palestine*, by Dr. Michael Prior, and *Israel's Anti-Civilian Weapons*, by John Mahoney, © 2000.

The Carter Institute in Atlanta, Georgia, for permission to reprint the article by Former President, Jimmy Carter, entitled *For Israel, Land or Peace*, © 2000.

The *Washington Report on Middle East Affairs* for permission to include sections of articles it has published.

Jews for Justice in the Middle East, for permission to quote from its two publications, *The Origin of the Palestine-Israel Conflict*, and *The Israeli Occupation: Background and Analyses of the Current Conflict*.

Harry Wendt, for permission to use *The Goals of Zionism in the Light of Christian Scriptures*, © 2002.

Dr. Kenneth E. Bailey for permission to include his poem *Resurrection* in the final section of this book.

CONTENTS

FOREWORD 1

ISRAEL, YESTERDAY AND TODAY 8
    Erich Renner

MODERN ISRAEL: PAST AND FUTURE 26
    Dewey M. Beegle

CONFRONTING THE BIBLE'S ETHNIC CLEANSING
    IN PALESTINE 40
    Michael Prior, C.M.

ISRAEL'S ANTI-CIVILIAN WEAPONS 63
    John Mahoney

FOR ISRAEL, LAND OR PEACE 86
    Jimmy Carter

THE GOALS OF ZIONISM IN THE LIGHT OF
    CHRISTIAN SCRIPTURES 94
    Harry Wendt

HELPS FOR DEVELOPING AN INFORMED
    WORLD-VIEW 120
    Harry Wendt

EPILOGUE 136

Foreword

My pilgrimage in relation to thinking through the situation in the Middle East began in 1970 while I was pursuing graduate work in biblical studies in St. Louis, MO. In September of that year, Dr. Ken Bailey and his family moved into the next-door apartment, and the Wendts and the Baileys have kept in touch ever since. Dr. Bailey, a Presbyterian theologian and now retired in New Wilmington, PA, taught biblical studies for forty years at Catholic and Protestant seminaries in Cairo, Beirut, Bethlehem, and Cyprus. Despite "retirement," he continues to do research, write, and lecture in various parts of the world.

The Baileys lived in Beirut in Lebanon for twenty years where Dr. Bailey taught at the Near Eastern School of Theology. They remained in Beirut during that horrendous period in 1982 when the Israeli army invaded Lebanon and destroyed much of its capital city. In 1983, Dr. Bailey gave a lecture in the United States in which he described his family's experiences during the invasion. He shared information of a kind that never makes its way into the U.S. media. The lecture was recorded, and Dr. Bailey provided me with a copy of the tape – which I listened to twice while flying across the Pacific to conduct seminars in Australia. That recording moved me greatly, and influenced me to learn more about the situation in the Middle East.

In the lecture, Dr. Bailey told how, when the Israeli invasion of Lebanon got under way, the people in southern Lebanon fled north ahead of the invading army. However, when they got to the Litanni River, Lebanon's major waterway in the southern part of the country, they found that all the bridges across the river had been destroyed. Two to three miles of cars lined up at a place where the people hoped that some kind of temporary bridge could be erected to enable them to cross the river. While the Lebanese people were waiting, Israel jets swooped in and killed virtually all of them.

The evening after this slaughter, Dr. Bailey and his wife attended a gathering in Beirut attended, among others, by reporters for CBS from the United States who had filmed the massacre. The reporters were in a state of shock. They said that though they had filmed events in Vietnam, they had seen nothing there as horrifying as the slaughter of the previous day. Furthermore, they expressed deep frustration in that, though they had risked their lives to photograph what had transpired, they knew that not one second of it would ever be shown on American TV – which it was not. The reporters stated that anything that showed Israel's military actions in a negative light would never be shown "back home" – a state of affairs that still prevails to a large degree.

Dr. Bailey went on to describe how the Israeli forces fired American-made smart bombs into bomb shelters and dropped American-made implosion bombs on buildings causing them to crumble as did the Twin Trade Towers, killing thousands of people. He told how colleagues became emotionally distraught while counting hundreds of heads in the destroyed bomb shelters and feeling utterly helpless when the cries of those trapped under collapsed buildings grew more faint and ceased after about three days. He also told how the Israeli armies did not actually enter Beirut to engage in close combat, but stayed some miles from the city and blew it to pieces with U.S. made weapons. In that horrendous war, 318 Israeli fighters were killed. However, 18,000 Lebanese were killed and 30,000 were injured.

Dr. Bailey is totally informed about what has been happening, and continues to happen, in the Middle East. I consider it an honor that he has given me permission to use a poem that he wrote as the Epilogue to this publication.

My pilgrimage continued when a Presbyterian pastor who attended one of my seminars put me in touch with his uncle, Edwin Wright. Wright served in the U.S. Army Middle East Command and on the General Staff, with the rank of Lieutenant Colonel, from 1942 to 1945. After the war, he joined the Department of State, holding several positions in the Bureau of Near East, South Asian and African Affairs. From 1955 to 1966, he was the Assistant Dean of the Foreign Service Institute and Professor of International Relations. He lectured repeatedly at, for example, the Johns Hopkins University School of International Studies, the National Army and War Colleges, the Naval and Military Academies and countless other government schools and private universities. He was decorated with the Legion of Merit and the Department of State's Superior Merit Award.

Though I never met Wright, during the early 1980's we talked by phone from time to time – and he sent me a copy of a book he had written for The Harry S. Truman Library in Independence, Missouri. The book, entitled *The Great Zionist Cover-Up*, challenged me greatly – and still does. It helped me understand the origins of the Zionist movement, its continuing history, and the influence that it continues to have in the United States. Among other things, Wright summarized the Zionist dogma according to the theories and practices of Herzl, Weizmann, Ben-Gurion, Meir and other Zionist leaders:

> **One:** The Gentile world is by nature anti-Semitic and will eventually either destroy or assimilate the Jewish people.
>
> **Two:** It is imperative that <u>ALL</u> Jews leave their homes in Exile and return to an exclusive Jewish state in Eretz Israel – the Land of Israel – restoring the ancient Kingdom of David and Solomon within its biblical boundaries, euphemistically called "The Jewish Homeland."
>
> **Three:** To protect the purity of the Jewish race – the Chosen People called "Ha Kehilla Ha Kadosha" – all non-Jews must be expelled, or if they refuse, they must live under laws and a psychological conditioning that will create a wall of separation between "the sacred community" and the Goyim – a phrase taken from the Torah, loaded with disdain and contempt.
>
> **Four:** Inasmuch as the scattered Jewish community lacks political unity and power, some foreign power must be persuaded to adopt the Zionist program. Here the <u>End</u> (a large Sovereign Exclusive Jewish State) justifies the <u>Means.</u> No Foreign Power will accept the above Zionist dogmas, so it will be necessary to camouflage the Zionist goals and methods of propagation by the use of humanitarian and emotional slogans. This will involve manipulation, propaganda, promises and threats, misinformation and deceit. Those Jews in high positions and influence in foreign states must be captured to become Zionist agents and thus further the Zionist program. Otherwise, as Herzl states, they are anti-Semitic and will be assimilated. Here the story of Esther is the biblical model.

Wright also quoted a statement by Dr. Israel Eldad, a fanatical follower of Theodor Herzl (*The Times of Israel*, August 29, 1969):

> Israel is the Jews' land – <u>not a land of Jews.</u> It may have, at one time, been a land of Arabs but it never was an Arab land. <u>Israel was the Jews' land even when no Jews resided in it.</u> It was never the Arabs' land, even when all its inhabitants were Arab. Israel belongs to four million Russian Jews despite the fact that they

were not born here. It is the land of nine million other Jews throughout the world, even if they have no present plans to live in it.

Wright's book also describes the influence the Zionist lobby in Washington had on President Truman at that point in time when, in 1947, a vote was about to be taken in the United Nations concerning Palestine: "to divide or not to divide?" He writes:

> President Truman also records the "threats" he received from the "extreme Zionists," but he does not designate them by name. I can. In one instance the men who threatened him were a committee of Zionists headed by Emmanual Cellar (Democrat of New York), accompanied by Rabbi Stephen Wise, who told him that Zionists had persuaded Dewey to support the Zionist policy, and unless Truman beat Dewey to the Zionist line, they would urge Jews to contribute to Dewey's campaign and vote Republican. Representative Cellar pounded on Truman's table and ended - "we'll run you out of town." I was told this by one of the White House staff who witnessed the event – and had served in Egypt with me, so I knew him well.

By the time I read these statements, I had worked through the biblical narrative many times in the course of conducting seminars to train pastors, teachers and lay-leaders around the world to understand and teach the Bible's "big story." Doing this forced me to come to grips with the issues Michael Prior deals with in his splendid essay, included in this publication. Furthermore, I – an Australian – was becoming increasingly aware that many conservative Christians in the United States (perhaps 50-60 million) shared the opinion expressed by Jerry Falwell in *The Rebirth of America* (The Arthus S. DeMoss Foundation, 1986, p. 226):

> Several thousand years ago God told Abraham that out of his seed would come a great nation, more numerous than the stars of heaven and the sands of the seashore. God promised Abraham that through his seed all the families of the earth would be blessed. This is the Messianic Promise. Jesus Christ provided the fulfilment for that blessing. *Although all people are equally loved by God, Jews are God's chosen people. Palestine belongs to Israel. God deals with all nations in relation to how those nations deal with Israel.* (emphasis mine).

As time went by, I also made contact with the publishers of *Washington Report on Middle East Affairs* (*WRMEA*) and *The Link*. They and their publications have provided information that never makes its way into the U.S. media; information about these publications is given in chapter six. For example, *WRMEA* informed me that President Begin of Israel had given Jerry Falwell a twin-engine jet, valued at about two or three million dollars, for his continuing support for Israel. And because the U.S. to date has given Israel about ninety billion dollars, it was actually the American people who paid for that jet.

[Those who wish to know more about the kind of moral and spiritual endorsement that Falwell and his colleagues provide for Israel are encouraged to read Grace Halsell's *Forcing God's Hand: Why Millions Pray for a Quick Rapture – And Destruction of Planet Earth:* Washington D.C., Crossroads International Publishing, 1999. Halsell's book is available from *WRMEA*; see chapter 6 for its address and phone number. In *The End of Days*, leading Jewish journalist, Gershom Gorenberg, writes revealingly about the hopes embraced by some Jews, some evangelical Christians and some Muslims with regard to the "end times," and reveals why, even in times of peacemaking, these views continue to be a powerful catalyst for combat (New York: The Free Press, 2000).]

My concerns with regard to the situation in the Middle East have prompted me to do a lot of reading and to offer this publication – an improved and expanded version of an edition published in 1983.

I wish to emphasize that, in producing this book, I write as one who is concerned about the paths along which Zionism is leading the United States. I am not anti-Semitic. I have numerous Jewish friends, including some involved in the "Peace Now" movement in Israel, and others involved in the "Jews for Justice" movement (from whose publications I quote below, in my major article, and in several chapters of this book). My concern is this: I believe it is essential that people in the United States study the history of the Zionist movement, and find out what has taken place in the so-called Holy Land these past one hundred years. It is essential that Christians understand the Bible's "big story" and the themes that weave their way through it, and face up to the fact that the goals of Zionism cannot be supported by appeals to the *Christian scriptures* (which consist of both the Hebrew Scriptures and the New Testament writings). And it is essential that the Christian community in the United States raises its voice to demand that justice prevail in the Middle East.

Since the ghastly events of September 11, 2001, the Arab world has often been portrayed in a negative light, and the impression given that many within its ranks are terrorists. This is simply not true, and the sad truth is that all nations have their radicals and terrorists. Furthermore, Christians in western nations need to know that there are many Christians in the Middle East. A recent estimate indicates that there are one million Christians in Iraq, about 170,000 in Israel and the West Bank, about 6-7 million in Egypt, about 300,000 in Jordan, and about 1.4 million in Lebanon.

In the December 3, 2001, issue of *The Banner*, Dr. Bastiaan Van Elderen, a retired professor of New Testament in seminaries in Grand Rapids and Amsterdam wrote:

> Western Christians must be concerned about these brothers and sisters in the Middle East, who find it difficult to comprehend that a sizable segment of the American evangelical community enthusiastically supports the state of Israel as fulfillment of biblical prophecy yet totally ignores the resultant suffering of fellow Christians. A theology that endorses policies that cause human suffering, especially that of brothers and sisters in Christ, cannot be reconciled with the biblical message of love, justice and equality.

As this publication seeks to show, the biblical passages the evangelical community uses to validate its support of Israel simply do not apply to present-day events. It would appear that many evangelical Christians who support Israel do so, not out of any great love for the Jews, but because they want to see the Jerusalem Temple rebuilt so that the events of the end time can take place and Jesus can return. Strange, is it not, that he who in the beginning managed to make all things, and did quite well in the incarnation and resurrection, needs a little human help in the "return process"? And even stranger that many who hope for Jesus' early return believe it will mean a joyous rapture for them, but agonies for those "left behind"?

Many Jews are anti-Zionist. One of Zionism's most outspoken critics, Henry Morgenthau, declared:

> Zionism is the most stupendous fallacy in Jewish history. It is wrong in principle and impossible of realization; it is unsound in its economics, fantastical in its politics, and sterile in its spiritual ideals. Where it is not pathetically visionary, it is cruel, playing with the hopes of a people blindly seeking their way out of age-long miseries.

In his book *The Decadence of Judaism in Our Time*, Moshe Menuhin (father of the violinist Yehudi Menuhin) states:

> Zionist Israel is dragging an innocent and unknowledgeable world into an apocalyptic nuclear world war, which is bound to happen soon, unless a just peace is imposed in the Middle East, and all stolen and conquered Arab lands and properties are returned to their lawful owners.

I am writing this prologue about three months after the horrendous events of September 11, 2001, when the New York World Trade Center was destroyed in a terrorist attack. Those events indicate that there might be some truth in Moshe Menuhin's statement. After all, though Osama Bin Laden and his associates gave several reasons why the events of September 11 took place, the United States' unquestioning support of Israel was on the list.

We do well to remember the Chinese proverb: "When a butterfly flaps its wings in China, it affects the weather patterns around the world." Crossways International offers this publication with the sincere prayer that it will provide insights into the history behind the continuing problems in the Middle East, and insights into the only Peace Plan that will ever work – in the Middle East and anywhere else.

Harry Wendt
President, Crossways International

Israel, Yesterday and Today
Erich Renner

The term "Israel" means different things to different people. Most of the differing definitions carry emotive overtones. In its basic meaning, Israel stands for the Jewish people.

For some, the term conjures up thoughts of God's activity with his "special people" of the Old Testament, and their role in the biblical account of salvation history prior to the coming of Jesus the Messiah.

For others, the term has political connotations, and is linked with the Jewish people as a national or political entity of modern times. As such, it arouses either bitter animosity, or intense support.

Some complicate the matter by mingling the religious and political aspects of the term. They link today's political Israel to the fulfilment of Old Testament prophecies and to the unfolding of God's plans for the "end time." In doing this, they weld the Jewish people to the land of Palestine — because of the latter's close associations with the past and present history of Israel.

The pages of history are filled with accounts of invasions, wars, and acts of religious and political violence as Jews and Gentiles, Christians and Muslims have battled to determine who is to own and control this strategically-situated stretch of land.

The questions and answers that follow probe *briefly* Israel's origins, and its contentious and stormy history. The goal is to throw light on the problems posed by Israel *yesterday and today*, and to give rise to informed, responsible Christian concern.

1. Where does the name Israel first appear in the Old Testament?

The name first occurs in Genesis 32, where Jacob was about to face his brother Esau, whom he had badly deceived 20 years earlier. At the brook Jabbok, God confronted Jacob and in the wrestling bout that followed (with God appearing in human form), Jacob was injured. Before leaving Jacob, God said to him, "You shall no longer be called Jacob, but Israel, for you have struggled with God and with humans, and you have prevailed."

Several points emerge from this incident. First, God chose the name, not Jacob. As most name-changing in the Old Testament denotes, the incident points to a change in the person's life and behavior from that point on. Second, by referring to themselves as "sons of Israel," Jacob's descendants were reminding themselves of God's intervention and confrontation with Jacob. In short, the name was first given in the context of a *reconciliation journey* by the patriarch Jacob. Its real setting was within the sweep of the redemption history begun by God with Abraham, Genesis 12:1-3

The term *Israel* occurs about 2,500 times in the Old Testament. Of that number, the name occurs within the term *sons of Israel* 637 times (see G. Gerlemann's article on Israel in the *Old Testament Theological Dictionary* by Jenni-Westermann). The term occurs 237 times in Numbers, and more than 400 times in Isaiah, Jeremiah and Ezekiel. It obviously has great significance in the Old Testament.

2. Is the name Israel found outside the Old Testament?

The oldest inscription on which the name *Israel* is found is the famous so-called *Israel stele* (stone inscription) from Thebes in Egypt (preserved today in the Egyptian Museum at Cairo). One of the songs sung to celebrate Pharaoh Merneptah's great victories over Canaan declares, "Israel is laid waste, his seed is not; Huru (*Greater Palestine*) is become a widow for Egypt." Though scholars debate whether the name is to be taken as referring to a people, or whether it is to be identified with an older sociological grouping, one thing is certain: By about 1220 B.C. the name Israel was being used outside the land of Palestine.

The most undisputed reference to Israel from extra-biblical sources appears in the famous *Mesha Inscription* of the Moabites, discovered in 1868 at Diban, east of the Dead Sea. The approximate dating of this stone, about 830 B.C., is defined by its reference to Mesha, king of Moab (see 2 Kings 3:4) stating, "I have triumphed over him (Omri) and over his house, while Israel has perished for ever."

3. When and how did Israel become the people of God?

Israel became a nation only when God broke into their bondage in Egypt and saved them from slavery. Because of, and beyond that act, their very existence and life depended totally on God. During their time in the desert, they learned that God was the supplier of all their wants and needs. Though Moses was their leader, he was that only because God had chosen him for that task.

At Mt Sinai, God entered into a God-people relationship with the Israelites by making a covenant with them: "I shall be your God and you shall be my people." The obedience to which the covenant commandments called the Israelites was to be a *response* to the relationship *God had established with them*. The covenant was not an agreement, with each side discussing and agreeing to the way things might be between them. Rather, God told the people who He was and what He had done for them, and then told them how they were to respond by obeying Him.

In short, the nation called Israel was born in the Sinai wilderness in a situation of grave danger. Deuteronomy states: "God sustained him in a desert land, in the howling wilderness waste; he shielded him, cared for him, guarded him as the apple of his eye" (32:10). Using allegorical terms, the prophet Ezekiel describes Israel's origins, "I passed by you, and saw you flailing about in your blood. As you lay in your blood, I said to you, 'Live! and grow up like a plant of the field'," 16:6,7.

As promised to the patriarchs, God gave the Israelites a land flowing with milk and honey — a paradise-like land when compared with the dangerous and death-like Egypt, Deuteronomy 8:1-10. God did not give them this land because He was impressed by their numbers; though Exodus 12:37 suggests that about two million Israelites might have fled from Egypt, Deuteronomy 7:7,8 suggest that they were the fewest of all people — perhaps a few thousand at most. Furthermore, this precious gift was not "deserved" because of any good quality they possessed, Deuteronomy 9:4-6. The narrative outlining their wilderness wanderings states that they continually murmured and rebelled against God. They were no better than the Canaanites whom they eventually drove from their land. The land became their dwelling place by grace alone. They were tenants, but never owners, Deuteronomy 28:15-68.

As long as they obeyed God's commandments and walked in his ways, loving and trusting in the Lord God as their only liberator (Deuteronomy 6:4), they were God's Israel, and the land was theirs *in trust*. They had no political or mythological claims to the land; it was theirs to use in the service of their God and their fellow-people. They were not to defile the land with idolatry and mixed worship; the fruits of the land were to go to God, and not to Baal. They were not to have anything to do with necromancy, witchcraft, consultation with the dead, for these were abominations to God. God alone was to be trusted and consulted; he provided them with his Word through his chosen prophets. Their kings were not to rely on horses in battle; their wars were the Lord's, Deuteronomy 20. God alone would provide the victory even in the face of overwhelming odds, Judges 7. When they waged a "holy war," they were to rely only on the power that God was able to provide them, and on the panic and confusion which he was able to send on Israel's enemies. Kings were to rule only by his favor and support, Deuteronomy 17:14-20.

Genesis 12:1-3 plays the key role in answering the question: "Why did God choose this people?" Here God's plan for all peoples is unfolded to Abraham. God did not abandon his rebellious creation, as he might have done. God did not totally destroy his creatures in the Flood, as he might have done. The imagination of the heart of humanity was constantly evil since the Fall, and God's complete rejection and destruction of his creatures would have been utterly just. But, in spite of human rebellion, God wanted fellowship with his world. Hence, after the events related to the tower of Babel (Genesis 11), God came to a man he chose from a pagan environment, and promised that through him blessings would flow *to* the nations (note: *to* the nations, not *from* the nations). This promise was repeated to the patriarchs who followed Abraham, and finally after a long and complicated history it reached its ultimate fulfillment in Jesus the Messiah of the New Testament. (See 2 Samuel 7; Isaiah 11 and 53; Matthew 1:1.)

4. Did Israel always remain God's People?

Many biblical scholars see the history of Israel recorded in the Old Testament as evidence of a failed mission — of the total failure of a people to live under their God. By and large, this is true — and is seen in the eventual tragic division of the land into two kingdoms (North and South — Israel and Judah) which took place after Solomon's reign (1 Kings 12); the idolatrous behavior of both northern and southern kings (despite the constant warnings of the prophets sent by God to halt the people's syncretism and sad political maneuvering), the false security which both kingdoms placed in their religious rites and holy places ("The Temple! The Temple! The Temple," Jeremiah 7:4; and "Peace! Peace!," 6:14) — these were just some of the evidences that Israel was not worthy of being God's People.

The prophet Hosea attacked Israel, the Northern Kingdom, some time prior to 721 B.C. Though his words were directed towards Israel, they were equally applicable to Judah. The prophet, drawing on his experiences in his marriage to a cult prostitute, announced to Israel that they were not God's people, but an adulterous people running after other gods, 1:2-8.

In the days of the Babylonian exile (597-538 B.C.), there was only a "remnant" left in the land that could rightly be called Israel. But, according to Amos (a southerner who preached to the Northern Kingdom about 750 B.C.), even that remnant was a sign that God had rejected his people — and not a sign that he was being merciful to them, as the "remainder theology" has often indicated.

Though God 's patience and love was great, yet there were also times when he had to warn, chastise, and reject Israel as his people. Prophets had to remind them that great privilege brought with it great responsibility. But because they had become self-secure and relied on institutions such as royalty, and the Temple and its worship, they had forfeited their claim to be God's people. While God again and again came to them, their propensity for leaving him was so strong that they incurred his anger, and brought disaster and ruin on their own heads, Hosea 11:1-7.

After the Judeans began returning from exile in Babylon in 538 B.C., they were never really a free people. Foreigners ruled them; and, although they were usually permitted to continue their worship practices in the Temple, they were never a free political power for any length of time, nor ever a unified people. Rather, they became splintered into movements (for example, the Maccabees, the pious in the land) and groups (the Sadducees and the Pharisees), which sometimes lived in an uneasy peace with one another as they tried to throw off their oppressors — the Persians, Greeks, Ptolemies, Seleucids and Romans. Even so, God continued to work throughout this complex history to ensure that His promise (Genesis 12:1-3) did not come to nothing. Through the "remnant" that held to his Word, God would fulfil his promise to heal all his creatures everywhere.

5. How did the coming of Jesus the Messiah affect the history of Israel?

In Matthew 1:1 (NRSV), we read, "An account of the genealogy of Jesus the Messiah, son of David, son of Abraham." These words have profound implications.

Two Judean kings were taken into exile in Babylon, Jehoiachin (597 B.C.) and Zedekiah, 587 B.C. Though Jehoiachin was still alive in Babylon in 560 B.C. (2 Kings 25:27-30), neither king returned to Jerusalem and Judah. The agony for the returning exiles was that though God had promised that David's dynasty would last forever (2 Samuel 7:), it now appeared to have come to an end. They gave vent to their grief in Psalm 89.

Hence, in his opening verse Matthew states that, in Jesus, the Jewish people got back the true descendant of David, who in turn was also the embodiment of the true descendants of Abraham.

The New Testament declares with great clarity and conviction that Jesus, born of the Virgin Mary, is the Messiah, whom God sent. In him, God wants to reconcile all people, both Jews and Gentiles, to himself. In other words, God once more came to his people, and spoke to them as never before. "Long ago God spoke to our ancestors in many and various ways by the prophets; but in these last days he has spoken to us by a son," Hebrews 1:1. The promise of seed made to Abraham, in whom all the families of the earth would be blessed, has been fulfilled in Jesus the Messiah. The new covenant prophesied in Jeremiah 31:31-34 was now established on the forgiveness of sins in Jesus the Messiah, the heart of the "good news" (Gospel) of the Kingdom of God. The peace with God which Jesus effected broke down the barriers between Jew and Gentile (Ephesians 2:14-22), and established the kingdom of peace, reconciliation, and love, of which Isaiah 11:6-9 and similar Old Testament prophecies had spoken.

One would be amiss to overlook the fact that, with the coming of Christ, the confrontation between God and his Old Testament People reached a frightening climax. The Old Testament had shown how Israel's history was punctuated by rebellions, back-sliding, idolatry, unfaithfulness, and rejection of a loving God who had rescued them out of Egypt and given them the promised land. Now, once again — in stark and terrible dimensions — their refusal to accept God's love and gifts was demonstrated by the rejection of the person of his Son and the demand for his crucifixion.

6. In what did the confrontation between Jesus and Israel consist?

To answer this question, a number of telling accounts in the New Testament can be used to good effect. In the story of the healing of the paralytic, Matthew (in chapter 9) records that Jesus said to the miserable sufferer: "Take heart, son; your sins are forgiven." Highly offended at this statement, the scribes said among themselves: "This man is blaspheming." Unimpressed by what Jesus claimed to be, and untouched by what he actually said and did, the Jews believed that he was blaspheming their God by forgiving sins — a right that was God's alone (the Hebrew word for "forgive," *salach*, is used only of God in the Old Testament). Narrowed down, the question uppermost in their minds was: "What shall we do with a man ("Joseph's son") who makes the claim that he is God?"

Another confrontation scene can be taken up at this point. John 8 shows that the Jews were convinced that Jesus was possessed of a demon. Their anger, however, burst into action, as they picked up stones to throw at him when he made the offensive claim: "Very truly, I tell you, before Abraham was, I am." That this was blasphemy for them was again expressed quite sharply in John 10:33: "It is not for a good work that we are going to stone you, but for blasphemy; because you, though only a human being, are making yourself God."

In the trial scene before Caiaphas, the same issue had to be faced by Jesus. Placed under oath, Jesus declared that he was indeed the Son of God — certainly not in the sense that the Jews claimed to be "sons of God" since they had been created and chosen by God (Matthew 3:9), but as the one who came from God, true God and true man.

In spite of Jesus' wooing of this people, and his attempt to gather them together (for they were "like sheep without a shepherd," Matthew 9:36), they refused to follow and accept him. On such occasions as when he turned a few loaves and fish into a banquet for them, they wanted to make him their bread-king; otherwise, he was misunderstood by them, rejected, and persecuted by this most religious people in the world. "He came to what was his own, and his own people did not accept him," as John 1:11 has it. Finally, amid accusations that Jesus was a dangerous usurper and rebel, a blasphemous attacker of all that was sacred (Matthew 24:2; 26:61), they nailed him to a cross as their final act of rejection and infamy.

The amazing and miraculous feature of this rejection by the people of Israel was that it was used by God for the saving work he had planned for the benefit of all people everywhere. The cruel crucifixion was, on the one hand, the lowest point in history, and, on the other, the most glorious moment in time, when God reconciled all his creatures to himself. So pleased was God with his Son's obedient suffering and sacrifice that on the third day he raised him from the dead. But even this demonstration of God's power and love in the resurrection was spurned by the majority of the Jews; they refused to believe in Jesus as the risen Messiah.

7. What were the results of this confrontation?

From the human, political viewpoint, it would be simple to say that it was the might of Rome which destroyed Jerusalem in the process of quelling the insurrections of the Jews. But the New Testament shows that the end of this city had been foretold by Jesus himself: "Indeed, the days will come upon you, when your enemies will set up ramparts around you and surround you, and hem you in on every side. They will crush you to the ground, and they will not leave with you one stone upon another; because you did not recognize the time of your visitation from God," Luke 19:43,44.

About A.D. 70, Jerusalem was razed, its beautiful Temple was completely destroyed, and many Jews were massacred. That event was a watershed in history; never again were sacrifices offered in a temple in Jerusalem. The rise of legalism and rabbinism came about as the result of this deep incision into their history. The Scriptures saw the end of Jerusalem and its cult as the just deserts for a people who had so bitterly and obstinately opposed and rejected God's own Messiah. Coupled with the destruction of their holy city, the people were scattered abroad in Asia and Europe, and completely lost their identity as a people. Their land had been taken, and their existence as a people was doomed forever.

8. According to St Paul, who is now the true Israel?

While not denying that God still has a history with his chosen Old Testament people, nevertheless, the true Israel for St. Paul is the Church of Jesus the Messiah, Romans 9:8. Members who have been baptized into his body constitute the real Israel, God's People. The children of promise (not of the Law) are the true people of God, made free from the old bondage of the law by Jesus through faith in him. Paul explains that neither circumcision nor uncircumcision makes for membership in God's People; the work of Jesus on the cross alone has brought about real fellowship with God, Colossians 3:11; Galatians 3:28,29; Ephesians 2: 11-18.

What, then, does he say about Jerusalem? The physical, geographical Jerusalem had its importance in redemptive history. In Old Testament times it was regarded as the "navel of the world," and, inasmuch as Jesus suffered, died, and rose there, Jerusalem will always remain precious in the memory of the people of God. But it is not the geographical "Mecca" of the Church. Only "the Jerusalem above" is "free, and she is our mother," as the Apostle Paul writes in Galatians 4:26. No rebuilt Jerusalem on earth can ever take the place of the new Jerusalem (which is heaven) in the believer's faith.

9. In Romans 9-11, St. Paul, who claims descent from the Jews, writes of Israel's rejection of the Messiah. What does he say about Israel's history?

In Romans 9-11, written by St Paul before the destruction of Jerusalem, the apostle wrestled with the problem of Israel's history. What was his problem?

Paul saw Israel as the chosen People of God; and yet they were not the People of God for they had killed the Prince of Life. For him, another question lay immediately adjacent to that: Has God abandoned them for ever? Paul's answer is clear: Israel's rejection of Jesus simply meant that the Gospel could now be released to the Gentiles (the non-Jews); the Jews' rejection of the Messiah was for the good of all other peoples in the world, Romans 11:11. What a remarkable assessment of Israel's history! Of course, the door for Israel was still open; and, even at that time, St. Paul believed that there was a remnant who were saved.

Then, in Romans 11:25,26, Paul writes those mysterious and sometimes grossly-misunderstood words: "Brothers and sisters, I want you to understand this mystery: a hardening has come upon part of Israel, until the full number of the Gentiles has come in. And so all Israel will be saved."

In the light of many other clear passages of Scripture, this last sentence cannot be made to mean that all Jews will one day be converted. Such a meaning was hardly in the mind of the apostle. But he was firmly convinced that the "disobedience" of Israel was not insuperable, and that the mercy of God on all people, whether Jews or Gentiles, was powerful enough to continue to include them in his history of everlasting love. That is why this remarkable piece of historical interpretation in the New Testament begins and concludes with a doxology, Romans 9:5 and 11:33-36. Indeed: "For who has known the mind of the Lord? Or who has been his counselor? Or who has given a gift to him to receive a gift in return?" (Romans 11:34,35).

What then is meant by "all Israel will be saved"? A recent commentator has put it well when he writes: "By God's wise governance of the history of the Gentile and the Jew, 'all Israel' (the whole of God's people from among the Gentiles) will be saved. There will be people of Israel, too, in that 'all Israel' at the end of days, for God's ancient promise to Israel holds." (For a fuller treatment of this difficult section, see the Concordia Commentary, *Romans*, by Martin H. Franzmann [St Louis: CPH, 1968], where a good explanation is given.

10. Why were there constant disputes between Jews and Christians in the early days of the Christian Church?

Most of the strongest debates and disputes between St. Paul and the Jews revolved around the understanding of the Law and the crucial question: "Who is Jesus?" Paul goes to great length to show the Jews that the Messiah of the Old Testament is none other than the Jesus of Nazareth. Many parts of the Gospels and the preaching in the Acts move strongly in that christocentric direction. Old Testament research of the early church centered chiefly in just this: The Law and the Prophets foretold the coming of Jesus the Messiah, the Savior of the world.

Elements of Jewish legalism (over-emphasis of the Law) entered the early Christian church so that a fierce confrontation took place between St. Paul and those who wanted to turn the Gospel into Law, and Jesus into a new Moses; see Galatians 3.

St. Paul was insistent that the Jews "when they hear the reading of the old covenant" have a veil over their minds "since only in Christ is it set aside. Indeed, to this very day whenever Moses is read, a veil lies over their minds; but when one turns to the Lord, the veil is removed," 2 Corinthians 3:14,15. In short, the Jews continued to interpret the Scriptures falsely — as they had already done in the days of Jesus, who told them "Moses wrote about me," John 5:46. Certainly Jesus' own disciples were not innocent of understanding the Scriptures in a legalistic way; only after the resurrection and Pentecost was the veil taken away from their eyes. Many Jews, however, continued in their false view of God's activity in the Old Testament, and therefore fell into work-righteousness and nomism.

11. Why have the Jews since New Testament times been a persecuted people?

History indicates various circumstances and reasons for the opposition to, hatred and persecution of the Jews. Among non-Christian societies, they were regarded at certain times as treacherous and disloyal people, because they refused to worship pagan gods. The words of Deuteronomy 6:4 were to determine their behavior; for them the Lord was the only God — to the exclusion of all other gods. The Jews were a scattered people even before the coming of Jesus; many of them were living in Alexandria, in other parts of Egypt, and elsewhere, e.g. Babylon. But after the fall of Jerusalem they had no real home-base, and hence were found in many parts of the then-known world, including Rome. Wherever they were found, it appears that some conflict, either explicit or latent, was as a result of their presence. However, because of the lack of information and historical facts, it is sometimes hard to know precisely how the Jews lived in certain societies.

Under the Muslims (after the 7th century) the fortunes of the Jews varied. On the one hand, they were allowed to flourish in North Africa and in Spain where their philosophers and thinkers reached a high peak of fame and excellence. But later in the Middle Ages it appears that intolerance set in, and the Jewish history became a tragedy also under Muslim rulers.

The conflict with Christians was even sadder and longer. Tragically, right from early Christian days the attitude to the Jews as those responsible for the crucifixion of Jesus (called deicide, or murder of God) hardened among Christians. Church fathers were sometimes harsh in their condemnations of the Jews, and the claim that Israel had forfeited their right to be God's chosen children in favor of the Church brought bitter conflict between Jews and Christians. Laws were passed by Christians which were often unjust, and the synagogue was regarded by some as little better than a brothel. Many of the Jewish meeting-places were destroyed in Africa, Asia, and Italy; popes denounced them in the so-called Dark Ages. While there were times when they were protected, generally speaking their lot was tragic to the extent that they sometimes could be expelled and "put to death at the whim of their owners."

Particularly in the days of the Crusades, the Jews were most savagely hated by the Christians. Many were massacred, being linked as "enemies of God" in the same breath with "the infidel Muslims." Not only reasons of religion were given for the destruction of Jews. Their money-lending practices were frowned upon at various times in history; they were blamed for diseases and plagues. Fierce opposition forced them into ghettos (separate hiding places) where many Jews lived in fear on the margin of society.

The later history of the persecution experienced by the Jews is too broad a subject to treat in detail here. But it can be said that Luther attacked the Jews too viciously in his writings (see Luther in "The Jews and Their Lies"), even though it is also a fact of history that he had defended them valiantly. Calvin also can be criticized for not allowing them to return to Geneva, from where they had been expelled in 1491. Some generations were more tolerant of them, but, on the whole, the Roman Catholic Church continued to oppose them right into modern times — until Vatican II revealed a distinct change of attitude.

The most obvious reasons for Luther's attack on the Jews can be given in the following. He was deeply disappointed that they, who had hailed him as their liberator early in his reformation work, now turned against him; he was warned of plots among Jews to poison him. But above all he was angry that they slithered out of their own Scriptures, the Old Testament, and this resulted in their blaspheming Jesus. Then, too, some of them tried to make sabbatarians out of Christians. In his final sermon preached on February 15, 1546, at Eisleben, Luther said, "Therefore you lords are not to tolerate them but to drive them out, but if they are converted and leave their usury and accept Christ then we shall gladly accept them as brothers and sisters."

In more recent times, the plight of the Jewish people has grown worse. Anti-Semitism in many places has blotted the pages of recent history, and has had its climax in the persecution and atrocities hatefully perpetrated in Nazi Germany when large numbers were driven out and countless others liquidated.

12. What are the reasons for the modern-day movement called Zionism, and why did it gain such impetus?

If the above factors are kept in mind, there is little wonder that the Jews longed and looked for:
    a. A land which they could call their own.
    b. A national identity which comes from owning modern territory in which they could develop nationally.

It is in this light that modern-day Zionism must be understood. It is a movement which had its beginnings in their early history, but which became vocal and articulate under the leadership of Theodor Herzl, a Jewish journalist in Vienna. He and his followers, meeting in 1897 in Basel, Switzerland, expressed openly the desire of Jews to return to Palestine as their "rightful, God-given home." It seems that Herzl was not fully convinced that it had to be that land, for he was prepared to settle for an English offer of 1903 to establish a home in Uganda. However, the great philosopher and thinker of the Jews, Martin Buber, contended that "Israel loses itself if it substitutes Palestine for any other land."

It was in the year 1917 (on November 2, to be precise) that the Balfour Declaration opened the doors of Palestine to a big influx of Jews. The British, who had fought and defeated the Turks, the occupiers of Palestine, committed themselves to the cause of the Jews and their determination to settle in Palestine (where 100,000 Jews had already lived since 1914).

After World War II, and the Nazi regime's attempt to solve the Jewish problem by liquidation, England relinquished her League of Nations mandate over Palestine, and the land was divided among Arabs and Jews by a decision of the United Nations. On May 14, 1948, amid great excitement, David Ben Gurion declared the existence of the State of Israel, and almost immediately 650,000 Jews were at war with 1,300,000 Arabs. Ever since, there has been strong and open hostility between Israel and the Arab world – with many in the latter being committed to the wiping out of Israel once and for all. Only in very recent times (since late 1977) has there been some hope for peace, largely due to the initiative of the leader of the Egyptians, Anwar Sadat.

13. Can modern-day events in the Middle East be linked with scriptural prophecy and fulfillment about the people of Israel?

There have always been people who have interpreted the whole of the Scriptures in a completely literalistic sense. They have taken Old Testament (and New Testament) prophecies quite literally — even difficult passages like Ezekiel 38 and Revelation 20 — and made them a blueprint which defines political and social happenings in history.

Such people are particularly vocal and active at the present time, due to the very successful promotion of the writings of Hal Lindsey (especially *The Late Great Planet Earth*) and others, and to the wide circulation of the magazine, *The Jewish Hope*. As a result, many Christians have been deluded into believing that Old Testament prophecies actually refer to today's nation of Israel and contemporary political events; they have been deceived into believing that what is happening in the Middle East and elsewhere today has been known and planned by God as part of his saving will for the world.

Some go so far as to see in the nation of Israel the beginning of what they mistakenly understand as the fulfillment of Romans 11:26, "And so all Israel will be saved." They declare: The Jews — or, better, Israel — are a people back in their land which was promised to them by God in the Old Testament. Soon their wholesale conversion to Christianity will take place, and that will usher in the return of Jesus to this earth, where he will reign in glory for a thousand years.

Such crass millennialism, built on a false understanding of Ezekiel 38 (Gog and Magog) and of scriptural prophecy in general, must be seen for the spiritual danger that it is. It misinterprets the Scriptures, adulterates the Gospel, and undermines the Christian hope.

Christian people need to be made aware of such facts as the following:

   a. Many Old Testament prophecies — particularly passages like those found in Ezekiel (especially ch. 38) and in Daniel — are apocalyptic, and are quite difficult to interpret. Countless vain attempts have been made throughout the centuries to establish a meaning and interpretation which is universally acceptable.

The glib and easy solutions put forward by Hal Lindsey must be carefully countered by a thorough study of the texts in question — and that without any bias.

b. Predictions about the end of the world and the happenings which precede it have been found sadly wanting in the course of history. Christians are certainly to be watchful for the "signs of the times," but even their vision is often blurred and their judgments have proved faulty. It is a misuse of the Scriptures to use them as pieces in a jig-saw puzzle unfolding political events. Because much of the Old Testament prophetic section is couched in dreams, visions, and symbolic language, ready-made solutions are not to hand. To say, for example, as Lindsey does, "We believe that the Common Market and the trend toward unification of Europe may well be the beginning of the ten-nation confederacy predicted by Daniel and the Book of Revelation," is to stamp his own personal ideas on a difficult and mysterious part of Scripture.

c. One critic of Lindsey evaluates the situation well by saying: "By his emotional predictions he [Lindsey] devalues the richness of Scripture, engages in eschatological blackmail [hammers fear of fire and brimstone rather than of God]... No doubt those who read him and accept his predictions are in need of certainty. But we who acknowledge Christ's dominion are called to a heroism of faith apart from the certainties of men and their fantasies, however sincere," (Charles A. Sauer in *Interaction*, vol. 16, no. 4, April 1975, 20,22). This singularly sound and pungent statement deserves to be widely known, understood, and remembered.

Some of the falseness of such beliefs, and their great danger, will be seen as our final questions are taken up and answered.

14. Is the modern State of Israel to be identified with the Israel of the Old Testament?

The nation of Israel is certainly not God's People as the Old Testament knew it, even though it has claimed for itself that great biblical name, and has established itself in the geographical territory of Palestine. Using the Scriptures as a yardstick to measure the Jewish claim to the name Israel, the issue is clear.

Without developing each point fully, it is well to note the following:

a. The nation of Israel today does not live under the covenant and the will of God as expressed in the Old Testament *Torah*. Its worship is no longer centered in a Temple, where sacrifices were to be made to the living God; modern orthodox Jews must be satisfied with worship in synagogues. The Talmud (a code of the teachings of the rabbis put together in about AD 500) is used to support the idea that worship is acceptable to God in a spiritual sense without actual animal sacrifices (as is done in Jewish synagogues). But does such spiritualizing of worship really measure up to the demands of their Old Testament law?

b. Modern Israel has no similarity to the theocratic nation of Old Testament times. Any visitor to Israel today soon discovers that many of the Israelis are liberal Jews: they have little or no time for the traditional Jewish faith or the observance of the Mosaic law, which their orthodox fellow Jews still uphold.

c. The New Testament, as pointed out earlier, knows of a continuing Israel which is the Church, the Body of Christ. This the Jews of today strongly reject. Many orthodox Jews are still awaiting the coming of the Messiah. Others have even claimed that the Christian Church is the mission-arm of Israel and that Israel is with the Father and has no need of a Messiah to come to God — a claim which directly contradicts Jesus' word first spoken to the Jews: "No one comes to the Father, but by me," John 14:6.

d. Israel today is essentially a secular state, maintained largely by, and very much dependent on, the military power of the USA and England. It is concerned with a democratic way of life, religious neutrality, and its own material prosperity.

15. What should be the relationship between the Church and Israel of today?

a. Any attitude of self-righteousness or feeling of superiority by the Church toward Jewish people either in an official or a private capacity must be positively avoided and overcome. Although it was the Jewish nation which was active in the crucifixion of the Lord of the Church, the guilt of that event belongs to all people everywhere, including members of the true Israel.

b. Dialogue particularly with the religious elements among the Jews of today should take place wherever and whenever possible. Both church and synagogue share the same Scriptures in the Old Testament. This was clearly stated in the consultation on Jewish-Christian Confrontation held in Oslo in 1975: "The fact that both (namely, Jew and Christian) move forward from the same Old Testament starting-point is a constant reciprocal challenge for Christians and Jews."

c. Efforts should be made to invite citizens of the nation of Israel today, as well as Jews living elsewhere, to join the true Israel by means of him who is Israel's greatest son, and the only hope and peace for all people (Luke 2:32) — Jesus the Messiah, the Son of God.

d. All hatred of Jews and all anti-Semitism should be rejected and combated. God our Father is not anti-Semitic. He whose Son was born of Jacob's line, and prayed from the cross: "Father, forgive them" (Luke 23:34), cannot and will not despise this people with whom he has had a special history for the good of all people.

16. Has the Lutheran Church in Australia made any statements on the Jewish question?

Among its official writings, The Lutheran Church of Australia has a document containing a section "On Eschatological Matters" which contains three pertinent paragraphs:

> 6.a) We believe that, since God wants all people to be saved (1 Timothy 2:4), and because of Romans 11:1, God has not cast away "His people" and desires also all the descendants of Abraham, all Jews, to be saved (Romans 11:15);
>
> 6.b) We admit the possibility that a greater number of Jews may be converted in the last times; however, the expectation that a time will come when all descendants of Abraham on earth, all the Jews, will be converted to Christianity and thus be saved has no foundation in Scripture;
>
> 6.c) We declare it to be the bounden duty of the Church to protest against the persecution of the Jews, to proclaim the Gospel also to the Jews and to pray for them with the Church of all ages, "that God and our Lord may take away the veil from their hearts; that they may acknowledge Jesus Christ our Lord."

Pray for the peace of Jerusalem!

Modern Israel: Past and Future
Dewey M. Beegle

Though many conservatives within Judaism and Christianity point to Old Testament prophetic passages to validate the present existence of the nation of Israel, their use of the Old Testament is open to question. Even so, these conservatives will continue to embrace their beliefs.

The question is: How should Christians regard present-day Israel? This question confronts us with one of the thorniest problems of our time. What is the valid justification for Israel, and what are the prospects of its future?

The Justification for Israel

After the terrible Tsarist massacres of Jews in 1881, some Russian Jews went to Palestine where they formed agricultural settlements. The dream became a flicker because of illness, initial opposition from the ruling Ottoman Turks, and lack of financial support .

The French philanthropist Baron Edmond de Rothschild (1845-1943) came to the rescue. He provided financial aid and agricultural experts so that the colonists could become self-supporting. In addition he purchased thousands of acres in Galilee and Samaria. Much of this land was located in the swampy regions of the Esdraelon Valley and the Coastal Plain, and since malaria had been so prevalent, the Arabs had not settled there. They drained the swamps and made the area habitable.

The legal purchase and reclamation of land was the basis for the Jewish presence in Palestine, and it is this secular argument which validates the Israeli claim to part of Palestine.

Ishmael and Isaac

It is a common myth among conservative Christians to interpret the current difficulties between Arabs and Israelis as a prophetic continuation of the feud between Ishmael and Isaac. This is utter nonsense! At different periods over the last 1,200 years the two groups have lived together in Palestine and other Mediterranean countries. The differences and feelings between them have been no greater than those between neighboring nationalities elsewhere with varying customs and religious beliefs. During the Turkish rule (A.D. 1517-1917), in fact, children of neighboring Arab and Jewish families were considered brothers and sisters of each other.

The Jews and Arabs are no more monolithic than any other groups of human beings. People on both sides range from loving, sensitive persons all the way over to angry persons with evil intent, and there are just as wide-ranging points of view in each group. The present state of the struggle is due to extremists.

Cultural Zionism

The most praiseworthy type of Zionism is that which works for the preservation and development of the spiritual and cultural aspects of Judaism. One of the great men in this movement was Asher Ginzberg (1856-1927), known commonly by his pen name *Ahad HaCam*, "The One of the People." He believed that the renewal of Judaism had to occur through education and literature, and as a means to this end he was largely responsible for the revival of Hebrew as a living language. In 1889 he formed the *Bene Moshe* ("Sons of Moses") Association. In 1885, while Ginzberg was beginning his work, reform Judaism (under the leadership of Rabbi Isaac M. Wise) made its historic Pittsburgh Declaration:

> We consider ourselves no longer a nation, but a religious community, and therefore expect neither a return to Palestine, nor the restoration of a sacrificial worship under the Sons of Aaron, or of any of the laws concerning the Jewish State.

Many prominent Jews favored the spiritual, cultural type of renewal and they had the support of concerned, influential Gentiles. One of the latter was Arthur James Balfour, Foreign Secretary of the British government. On Nov. 2, 1917, he issued the Declaration which was to bear his name:

> His Majesty's Government view with favor the establishment in Palestine of a national home for the Jewish people and will use their best endeavors to facilitate the achievement of this object, it being clearly understood that nothing shall be done to prejudice the civil and religious rights of the existing non-Jewish communities in Palestine.

Balfour himself and other government officials declared that they understood "home" to mean a "spiritual or cultural center ."

Political Zionism

A far different kind of Zionism emerged in the 1890's. It yearned to form a state of Israel. The leaders of this point of view came largely from eastern Europe. During the French Revolution (1789) the ghetto walls of western Europe began to crumble. Napoleon furthered the process of forcing Jewish equality wherever his army was victorious. The story was different in eastern Europe, especially Russia and Poland. Terrible discrimination and slaughter resulted in a wave of 2,500,000 refugees coming to the United States in a few years after the 1881 massacres.

These events etched fear and hatred in the minds and hearts of many young Jews. Their experience convinced them of two things:

    a. A prejudice against Jews flows in the veins of every Gentile or non-Jew, a bias which can never be eradicated.

    b. In order for Jews to find their true identity, to use a modern expression, they must live together in an independent state with freedom to determine their own future.

One can readily understand why they came to such conclusions, but that does not validate their views as universal principles. Many Jews in western Europe and the United States found that there were considerate, loving Gentiles who would allow them to be themselves and worship as they saw fit. The experiences of Jews in eastern Europe made it impossible for them to believe that such conditions were possible.

Zionists Herzl and Weizmann

The father of political Zionism was Theodor Herzl (1860-1904). In 1896 he published his book *Der Judenstaat* (The Jewish State), a book which relied heavily on books by Hess and Pinsker, Eastern European Jews. A year later at Basel, Switzerland, Herzl convened the first Zionist Congress. But difficulties within the ranks broke his health and he died in 1904. The new President, David Wolfssohn, favored "diplomatic Zionism" similar to Herzl's approach, but the Russian Jews demanded "practical Zionism," that is, the immediate colonization of Palestine. In 1911 a Zionist office was established in Jaffa and the city Tel-Aviv was founded just to the north.

The zealous Zionist Chaim Weizmann (1874-1952), saw that Great Britain was the most likely nation to accept the Zionist dream and so he left Russia in 1904 and immigrated to England. There he worked through many influential people who were sympathetic to Jewish interests.

In December 1916, when the tide of World War I turned against the western Allies, Weizmann made his trump move. He offered Prime Minister Lloyd George the support of the Jews (even in Russia and the United States) on condition that the British agree to facilitate a national home in Palestine. In his original draft of the agreement, Weizmann specifically referred to Palestine as "*the* national home for the Jewish people," and he spoke of the "reestablishment of the country."

A National Home in Palestine

But the British had already promised the Arabs that, for their help, Palestine would become independent after the War. Therefore, Balfour revised the draft to read "*a* national home for the Jewish people." Weizmann was disappointed with the "painful recession" from his proposal of "Palestine as *the* national home," yet he and his fellow Zionists persuaded France, Italy, and the United States to go along with the declaration.

Moreover, Balfour made explicit his understanding of "home" as "a cultural or spiritual center" by adding the strict condition, "it being clearly understood that nothing shall be done to prejudice the civil and religious rights of the existing non-Jewish communities in Palestine." The expression "non-Jewish" was a rather ironic way of referring to the Arab and Christian communities, especially since in 1917 the Jews represented only 8% of the population of Palestine.

The British Mandate

The next crucial step in the Zionist dream was in 1922 when the League of Nations, without United States participation, authorized the British Mandate of Palestine. Behind the scenes activity resulted in Article IV, which authorized the "Zionist Agency" as the appropriate "Jewish Agency" for the purpose of "advising and cooperating with the administration of Palestine" in connection with the Jewish National Home and the interests of Jews in Palestine.

At no time did the agency consider itself to be in an advisory or cooperative role. The Zionists determined, regardless of the wording of the Balfour Declaration, to make Palestine "the national home for the Jewish people." The British were no match for them and since there was no Arab agency, the rights of the Arabs were jeopardized on every hand. Inasmuch as absentee landlords in Lebanon and Syria were cut off from their property in Palestine by the international boundaries between the British and French Mandates, the Jewish Agency was permitted to buy the land at bargain prices. Furthermore, thousands of Arab tenant and farm workers were evicted from the newly acquired land in order to make room for Jewish settlers from Europe. Compensation for the evicted Arab families was very small, sometimes as low as $10 per family.

By 1930 the British government took notice of the Arab pleas and Mr. Ramsay MacDonald decided to control Jewish immigration to Palestine. Weizmann, then President of the World Zionist Organization, protested and threatened to resign. The resultant political pressure forced MacDonald to desist and again the Zionists had free reign in Palestine. When ruthless Adolf Hitler came to power in Germany the flow of Jewish immigrants increased drastically and by 1935 the Jewish population of Palestine had risen to 30%.

Civil War in Palestine

In 1936 war broke out between the Arabs and the Jewish population. Three years of suffering and frustration awakened the British government to the necessity of establishing new ground rules for the settlement of Palestine. In 1939 a "White Paper" set forth an equitable solution to the problem. After a ten-year interval Palestine would become an independent binational state with Arabs and Jews sharing the government and protecting the interests of each other. Immigration of the Jews was to continue for five years at 15,000 annually, but sale of Arab lands to the Jewish Agency was to be restricted.

Unfortunately, the forces of history conspired against this excellent proposal. The atrocities of the Nazi gas chambers resulted in a flood of refugees and the British, fighting for their own lives against Germany, were too weak to cope with the situation.

While the private Jewish police force *Haganah* ("Defense") carried on its normal protective functions, more radical groups stepped up the fighting in Palestine. In 1942, for example, Menachem Begin, a Polish Jew, formed the *Irgun Zvai Leumi*, ("National Military Organization").

One of its main activities was attacking British soldiers and officials. Inasmuch as the King David Hotel in Jerusalem was the Secretariat for the Palestinian Government, it housed a number of British officials along with some Arabs and Jews. In July, 1946, Begin and his *Irgun* blew up the south end of the hotel, killing many people.

The "hate Britain" campaign reached its peak in 1947 when the Zionists loaded 4,554 Jewish refugees on the old "President Warfield," which had been renamed "S.S. Exodus," and attempted to take them to Haifa. The British seized the vessel as a flagrant violation of regulations attempting to control the flow of immigrants, and the passengers were returned to France on three British vessels. When the refugees refused to disembark they were taken to Hamburg, Germany, and forcibly removed. The hysteria evoked by this incident brought the situation full circle to the conditions of the Jewish revolts in A.D. 66-70 and 132-135. As zealot groups became more violent, the oppressive measures of the rulers were increased. Except for the British replacing the Romans, the situations were much the same.

Displaced Persons

During the fateful years of World War II the expression "Displaced Person" (DPs) was seared on the conscience of humanity. The pathetic condition of the DPs evoked great empathy and the guilt of western civilization for having permitted Hitler to rise to power and to carry out his insane brutalities demanded that action be taken to alleviate the misery.

President Franklin D. Roosevelt tried quietly to find homes for the European refugees in the United States, Britain, Canada, Australia, and South America. Many of the DPs wanted to immigrate to these countries, especially the United States, and these nations had the room and capability of absorbing most of them. But Roosevelt found such bitter opposition to the idea he dared not push it through.

The reward for his interest in the welfare of the refugees was the label "anti-Semitic." In truth, the anti-Semites were the Zionists themselves because they did not really have the ultimate concern of the DPs at heart — they only wanted to use them as pawns to achieve the dream of a Jewish State. Although Zionist opposition to the Roosevelt idea was cloaked under the righteous indignation of humanitarianism, the real reasons were:

1. More Jews were needed to populate Palestine.
2. It would be exceedingly difficult to raise money for Palestine if most of the Jews were settled elsewhere.

Proof of these underlying motives came to the surface in 1947 when William G. Stratton sponsored a bill to admit DPs up to the limit of the accumulated unused immigration quotas for the war years. Passage of the bill would have permitted about 400,000 refugees to come to the United States. Here was the ultimate test of Zionist motivation. Their powerful lobby in Washington, usually so vocal, was deathly silent.

Only Gov. Herbert Lehman of New York had the courage to speak in behalf of the bill. Stratton was shocked at the lack of support, but he did not know that the President of the Zionist Organization of America had recently said, "I am happy that our movement has finally veered around to the point where we are all, or nearly all, talking about a Jewish State." The message of the Pittsburgh Declaration of 1885 was drowned out by the emotional propaganda of the Zionists and many Reform Jews were sucked into the vortex of the massive whirlpool.

Palestine and the United Nations

Conditions became so chaotic in Palestine, the British finally despaired and took the issue to the newly formed United Nations Organization. On April 28, 1947, a Special Session was called to consider the facts. In general, the Arabs favored a binational state whereas most of the Jews were yearning for a Jewish State.

An outstanding exception was Dr. Judah Magnes, President of the Hebrew University of Jerusalem. He had prayed and worked for a binational state with "understanding and cooperation between Jew and Arab." In addressing the 23rd Convocation of the University he spoke of "Zionist Totalitarianism" which was attempting to bring "the entire Jewish people under its influence by force and violence." With amazing courage he added, "I have not yet seen the dissidents called by their rightful names: killers — brutalized men and women."

But Dr. Magnes was not permitted to express himself during the UN debate because Zionists, who were zealously at work behind the scenes, had seen to it that only the Jewish Agency would be permitted to speak for Palestinian Jews. In order for the Magnes point of view to get before the public, it was necessary for Dr. Albert Einstein to issue a statement through the press.

The question whether Palestine was to be partitioned or to become a binational state turned the UN debate into "pressure-cooker politics." A two-thirds vote was required and since 12 of the smaller nations were for a unified Palestine, a telegram from 26 pro-Zionist United States Senators was sent urging them to vote for partition. General Carlos Romulo made an eloquent appeal for a binational state, but with six bills involving the Philippines pending before the Senate, the Philippine delegation regretfully shifted its vote. Of the 12, only Greece voted for unification. That shift of 11 votes turned the tide for partition.

A presidential election was to be held in 1948 and most of the politicians were courting the Jewish voters. President Truman was in favor of the Trusteeship Plan for Palestine, but he was warned that if he wanted to keep the Jewish vote he would have to recognize Israel. The "heat" was too much for Harry and "he got out of the kitchen" by announcing at 6:11 p.m., May 14, 1948, that the United States recognized the new State of Israel. At that very moment the UN was in session and the United States delegation, which had *not* been informed of the recognition, was pressing for the Trusteeship Plan. Other delegations got the news first and Ambassador Austin, head of the delegation, was justly dumbfounded and outraged when he heard how the White House had double-crossed him. As one UN delegate remarked, "The representatives of the USSR and Poland were better informed on events in Washington."

The Partition of Palestine

In Palestine the Jewish militant groups had stepped up their acts of intimidation and violence. Their motivation was twofold:

1. To remove as many Arabs as possible from the area designated by the partition plan for the Jews.
2. If possible, to gain more territory than that allowed by the plan.

The *Irgun's* (a Zionist military group) radio unit broadcast in Arabic that typhus, cholera, and other diseases would break out among the Arabs, and the *Haganah* (another military group) hinted dire consequences if the Arabs did not move.

The emigration was not fast enough, however, therefore the *Irgun* selected Deir Yassin as an example. The little Arab village, west of Jerusalem, was encircled by Jewish settlements, and on April 9, 1948, the terrorists swept in and literally butchered 254 men, women, and children. Loudspeaker vans of the *Haganah* drove through Arab settlements reporting "Arabs are fleeing in terror and fear." "The road to Jericho is open," the vans noted; "flee for your lives."

The late venerable Christian missionary Bertha Vester reported later that some of the broadcasts said, "Unless you leave your homes, the fate of Deir Yassin will be yours."In remarkable contrast to these heinous deeds, Shabetai Levi, the late Mayor of Haifa, with tears in his eyes begged the Arabs to stay. But the *Haganah* countered his plea by furnishing transportation for the fearful Arabs.

There were still large pockets of Arabs within the borders of Israel and since these were considered an internal threat, Moshe Dayan and his columns started another exodus. They roared into Lydda (Lod) with tanks and trucks and began shooting up the town. This incident and a similar one at Ramleh, south of Lod, resulted in 30,000 Arabs fleeing for the Arab-controlled sections of the hill country. Another pressure point was at Acre (Acco), north of Haifa, where an estimated 45,000 Arabs were driven out. As a result, the refugee camps near Nablus and Jericho became swollen, festering sores.

Devotion to Palestine

Various ideas were proposed to relieve the suffering of the camps, but the refugees refused to accept money for their land or to move elsewhere. The exceedingly pragmatic mentality of western culture, especially the United States, could not understand the attitude of the refugees. "Why not be sensible and accept money ," so it was argued, "in order to buy land in another Arab country?" "With all the land owned by the surrounding Arab countries, why not re-settle the Arabs of Palestine and thus free for the Jews the little piece of land which is rightfully theirs?" But this line of reasoning disregarded the biblical evidence and it failed to understand the Arab point of view. To accept money for the appropriated land would, in the eyes of the refugees, amount to an admission that the Jews were right in taking the Arab land. Moreover, the western mentality failed to see that Arab devotion to a particular piece of land was as tenacious as that of the Jews.

The fundamental issue, in short, was the struggle over the same piece of land, and the basic question was "Why should the Arabs have to pay for the sins of Hitler and other Europeans?" Westerners were too involved with their guilt and sentimentality to ask this question, and to this day they have not been able to give a valid answer.

Citizens of Israel

The new State of Israel elected as Prime Minister the staunch Zionist, David Ben-Gurion. He contended that all Jews should immigrate to Israel, and as the official spokesman for Zionism he made it clear that Jews who did not do so were unfaithful to the cause. Under his pressure, the Israeli *Knesset* (Parliament) passed the "Nationality Bill" on July 14, 1952. The bill declared that every Jew, regardless of nationality and location, automatically could become a citizen of Israel.

But American Zionists did not rush to Israel, and Ben-Gurion was quick to point up the gap between their theory and their practice. Thoughtful Jews of other countries sensed that the bill was another Zionist tactic to increase the flow of immigrants, and they rejected the imposed allegiance to Israel because dual allegiance was impossible for them. Young Jews from other countries, especially the United States, took sentimental journeys to Israel for extended visits, but the glamor of the Zionist dream wore off and they returned home.

Anti-Semitism

Any open discussion of Zionist activities is usually labeled "anti-Semitism." In the first place, the designation is a misnomer. The Hebrew Bible is quite clear that the Arabs are sons of Abraham and thus Semites too. Many American Jews have observed that the Arabs look more Semitic than the European Jews. There is a good historic basis for this judgment.

Many so-called Jews are biologically the descendants of peoples who were converts to Judaism (for example, the Khazars, in what is now southwestern Russia, converted to Judaism in A.D. 740 when their leader Bulan became a proselyte). Israelis have all types of physical features and colorings, and in many instances these Jews resemble the non-Jewish peoples among whom they formerly lived. The Oriental (Arab-speaking) Jews are far more authentic racially than their European counterparts. In truth, therefore, Judaism is a religion or a point of view and it has no primary basis in race.

Far more serious than the inaccuracy of the term "anti-Semitic" is the fact that it is a vicious psychological tool. Every minority has suffered from injustice and had reason to label its misery, but somehow the racism of Europe high-lighted the concept of "anti-Semitism." Herzl said, "Anti- Semitism had grown and continues to grow — and so do I."

It will be recalled that the basic concept of Zionism has been the belief that the indelible prejudice of non-Jews makes it impossible for Jews to be assimilated in any Gentile nation or culture. Herzl's statement was an unintentional admission that Zionism has a stake in racism.

From the very start, Zionism has thrived on prejudice and what its advocates have never been willing to face, then or now, is that the seeds of prejudice which they claim to find in non-Jews are more often than not the projections of their own minds. People with martyr complexes invariably interpret actions of others as being inimical to their own interests, and this is especially true in the case of Jews with ghetto mentalities. The tragedy of this situation is that valid criticisms are discounted and therefore all remedial measures are nullified. *When any one person or group of people puts itself beyond the reach of criticism, it is committing psychological and ethical suicide.*

The late Dr. Magnes was absolutely correct when he regretfully noted that Zionism had increased anti-Semitism rather than diminished it. Without the expression "anti-Semitic" the cause of Zionism would hardly have succeeded. The British writer Ian Gilmour has stated the truth in one sentence: "Zionism aggravated the disease it professed to cure."

Anti-Zionism

But when a pro-Zionist rabbi declares, "Anti-Zionism is a new guise for anti-Semitism," one can be sure that the old psychological tool has been re-sharpened for use in the present situation. The fact that Semitism and Zionism are equated is proof of the obtuse Zionist mentality. The goals and methods of the Zionists are poles apart from the spirit of true Judaism. Such courageous anti-Zionist Jews as Rabbi Elmer Berger and Dr. Alfred M. Lilienthal have been saying this for years, but the reward for their labors has been the tag "traitor." *The Arabs and those who seek justice in their behalf are not anti-Jewish: they are simply anti-Zionist.*

The same can be said for other courageous Jews. Henry Morgenthau, Sr., one of the most outspoken critics, declared:

> Zionism is the most stupendous fallacy in Jewish history. It is wrong in principle and impossible of realization; it is unsound in its economics, fantastical in its politics, and sterile in its spiritual ideals. Where it is not pathetically visionary, it is cruel, playing with the hopes of a people blindly seeking their way out of age-long miseries.

In his book *The Decadence of Judaism in Our Time*, Moshe Menuhin (father of the violinist Yehudi Menuhin) states:

> Zionist Israel is dragging an innocent and unknowledgeable world into an apocalyptic nuclear world war, which is bound to happen soon, unless a just peace is imposed in the Middle East, and all stolen and conquered Arab lands and properties are returned to their lawful owners.

Who Is Responsible?

Space does not permit a survey of events since 1952. Enough has been said to indicate the basic pattern of events. The situation of Israel and the Arabs has been much like feuding boys in a classroom. Rather than hitting his foe with his fist or a ruler, the psychologically astute school boy whispers innuendoes and makes secretive grimaces which escape the teacher. Finally in desperation the object of the psychological attack flails back only to be detected and punished.

The Israelis have pleaded innocence and managed to convince most of the world that the Arabs are the aggressors when many times, in fact, the Arabs were provoked into action by the sly, aggressive ways of the Zionists. Nasser's rhetoric in 1967 inflamed the volatile Arabs with dreams of "holy war," but *they were never really ready to fight one.* However, it gave the Israelis the perfect excuse for catching the Egyptians with their planes down.

The focus on Zionist activities is not intended to absolve the Arabs. They have done their share of cruel, harmful things, but many of these acts were brought on by festering hatred over loss of relatives and homes due to Israeli actions. The Israelis make the same claim, of course, and then inflict more than an "eye-for-an-eye" retribution in order to teach the Arabs a lesson. Sooner or later they may come to realize that "those who take the sword will perish by the sword."

The Israeli claim of innocence cannot stand up in the light of the long, aggressive history of the political Zionists working from a position of prestige, power, and financial backing. *The major responsibility for the boiling pot in the Near East rests with them.* Most certainly extremists have kept the war pot boiling, but there is no ethical justification for calling bitter Palestinian guerillas and hijackers "beasts" when Menachem Begin and his fellow butchers of Deir Yassin are praised as "heroes" and elected to high office.

Election to Responsibility

Conservative Christians never seem to tire of sentimentalizing the idea of Jews as "the chosen people." They were indeed chosen and through no merit of their own. But *their election was for service and responsibility, not favoritism.* The prophet Amos warned, "You only have I known of all the families of the earth; therefore I will punish you for your iniquities," 3:2.

Because of their awful experience in Egypt, the Israelites were instructed that when they came into power in the land of Canaan they were to protect and treat justly the helpless groups: the orphans, widows, sojourners (aliens without voting rights). Many of the Zionists have been atheists. They gave up on the idea that the Messiah would come and deliver them from their miseries, and so they decided to take matters into their own hands. But the God of Israel did not die with their rejection, and sooner or later the Zionists will have to stand before him and account for their actions.

The Peace that Could Be

There is probably more brain power per square meter in Israel than in any other country of the world. The Jews have the advantage of centuries of education and the backing of millions of powerful, wealthy friends, both Jew and Gentile. They have rights in Palestine and the major powers should guarantee these rights. *All talk of pushing the Israelis into the Mediterranean, whether rhetoric or not, must stop.*

On the other hand, Israelis have some responsibilities. They must forget the zealot's dream, shared by the dispensationalists, that Israel has the right to all the territory between Wadi-el-Arish and the Euphrates. They must quit dragging their feet and nitpicking at every issue.

Real peace will not come in the Near East until the Palestinian problem is solved. Not all those Arabs who were driven from their homes want to return to the land they used to occupy. But whether they return or not, "reparations" are due them for their material loss and years of suffering and frustration. The Israelis justly demanded and received "reparations" from Germany, and there is equally good reason why they and their friends should pay "reparations" to the Palestinians. The cost will be small compared to the millions wasted on massive defense. With peaceful borders there will be no need for 300% duty on imported items and two-thirds of the budget for military hardware. If the Israelis seek this kind of peace "with a whole heart," the Near East can begin to blossom like Eden. With open, friendly borders they could travel and see the fantastic sites of antiquity in the area. The Arabs need their "know-how" to help reclaim land which has been abused for centuries.

In the truest sense, the Arabs and Israelis need each other, and there are many warm-hearted people on both sides who long for the day that both groups can live and work together in peace. In his book *Israel Without Zionists*, Uri Avneri, the courageous Israeli, laments that such has not been the case:

> If only we had turned Israeli Arabs into true partners in the building of the land. If only our plans for development embraced Arabs and Jews together, without discrimination. If only the Arabs were represented in all walks of natural life — in the supreme court, in the national soccer team, in our embassies and in our delegations to the United Nations.

Once when pleading for justice in Israel, Avneri was bodily removed from his seat in the *Knesset*. Many more mediating voices are needed on both sides of the dispute.

Fear has dominated the lives of most Israelis and it is crucial that their gnawing fear and insecurity be healed. Recent history, however, has shown that threats and military action will never remove it. The most secure borders are friendly borders, but to secure them, acts of justice will have to drain off the festering pools of hatred which have accumulated over the last century.

The real solution is for each side to sense and understand the physical and psychological pain of the other side. The sight of numerals tattooed on Israelis is a frightening reminder of the death they escaped. Enough sorrow has occurred already without having any more innocent blood shed. Equally touching is the sight of Palestinians in Jordan looking with tearful eyes across the Jordan Valley to the area where they used to live. There must be a just solution to this complex problem!

President Anwar Sadat's visit to Israel was a startling breakthrough, and the Israelis and Arabs conferring in Egypt on Christmas Day was an impressive symbol of the peace that could be. The dream will come closer in reality if, in the spirit of Camp David, President Carter can convince the Israelis to withdraw completely from the West Bank, Gaza Strip, and Sinai areas. In a real sense, the Israelis have their future in their own hands. Across the centuries, Moses still pleads: "I have set before you life and death, blessing and curse; therefore choose life, that you and your descendants may live," Deuteronomy 30: 19.

Confronting the Bible's Ethnic Cleansing in Palestine

Michael Prior

It is mid-October 2000; to date, at least 98 Palestinians and 7 Jews have been killed, and over 3,000, mostly Palestinians, injured in the Holy Land's most recent unholiness. That's the math of it.

It is, however, the morality of it that has engaged me over the past quarter of a century.

I would have been spared some pain had I not undertaken significant portions of my postgraduate biblical studies in the land of the Bible. And although the focus of my engagement was "the biblical past," I could not avoid the modern social context of the region. As a result, my studying the Bible in the Land of the Bible provoked perspectives that scarcely would have arisen elsewhere.

For me, as a boy and young man, politics began and ended in Ireland, an Ireland obsessed with England. Much later I recognized that the history I absorbed so readily in school was one fabricated by the nationalist historiographers of a newly independent Ireland, who had refracted the totality of its history through the lens of 19th-century European nationalisms. Although my Catholic culture also cherished Saint Patrick and the saints and scholars after him, the real heroes of Ireland's history were those who challenged British colonialism in Ireland. I had no interest in the politics of any other region — except that I knew that Communism, wherever, was wrong. Anyhow, the priesthood beckoned.

My seminary courses on the Old Testament first sensitized me to the social and political context of theological reflection. We inquired into the real-life situations of the prophets, and considered the contexts of the Wisdom Literature. Beyond the narratives of Genesis 1-11 and Exodus, however, I do not recall much engagement with the Torah. The atrocities recorded in the Book of Joshua made no particular impression on me. The monarchy period got a generous airing, noting the link between religious perspectives and changing political circumstances. But just as I was not sensitive at that stage to the fact that Irish nationalist historiography had imposed a rigid nationalist framework on everything that preceded the advent of interest in the nation state, it never crossed my mind that the biblical narrative also might be a fabrication of a past, reflecting the distinctive perspective of its later authors.

Prior to the 5-10 June 1967 war, I had no particular interest in the State of Israel, other than an admiration for Jews having constructed a nation state and restored a national language. In addition to stimulating my first curiosity in the Israeli-Arab conflict, Israel's conquest of the West Bank, the Golan Heights, the Gaza Strip and Sinai brought me "face to face," via TV, with wider, international political realities. The startling, speedy, and comprehensive victory of diminutive Israel over its rapacious Arab predators produced surges of delight in me. And I had no reason to question the mellifluous mendacity of Abba Eban at the United Nations, delivered in that urbanity and self-assurance characteristic of Western diplomats, however fraudulent, claiming that Israel was an innocent victim of Egyptian aggression.

Later that summer in London, I was intrigued by billboards in Golders Green, with quotations from the Hebrew prophets, assuring readers that those who trusted in biblical prophecy could not be surprised by Israel's victory. Up to then, my understanding was that biblical prophecy related to the period of the prophets, and was not about predicting the future. The prophets were "forth-tellers" for God, rather than fore-tellers of future events. I was intrigued that others thought differently.

I was to learn later, in the 1980s and 1990s, that the 1967 war inaugurated a new phase in the Zionist conquest of Mandated Palestine, one which brought theological assertions and biblical interpretations to the very heart of the ideology that propelled the Israeli conquest and set the pattern for Jewish settlement. After two more years of theology, ordination, and three years of postgraduate biblical studies, I made my first visit to Israel-Palestine at Easter 1972, with a party of postgraduate students from the Pontifical Biblical Institute in Rome.

Seeing and Believing

The visit offered the first challenge to my favorable predisposition toward Israel. I was disturbed by the ubiquitous signs of the oppression of the Arabs, whom later I learned to call Palestinians. I was witnessing some kind of "institutionalized oppression" — I cannot recall whether 'apartheid' was part of my vocabulary at the time. The experience must have been profound since, when the Yom Kippur War broke out in October 1973, my support for Israel did not match my enthusiasm of

1967. I had no particular interest in the area for the remainder of the 1970s, but I recall watching on TV the visit of Egypt's President Sadat to the Israeli Knesset in November 1977, an initiative which would culminate in a formal peace agreement in Camp David in 1979. Things changed for me in the 1980s.

In 1981 I went with a party from my university to visit Bir Zeit University in the Israeli-occupied West Bank. Because the campus was closed by the military just before our arrival, carefully planned programs had to yield to Palestinian "*ad-hocery.*" Bir Zeit put a bus at our disposal, and equal numbers of its and our students constituted a university on wheels. I was profoundly shocked when I began to see from the inside the reality of land expropriation and the on-going Jewish settlement of the West Bank. I began to question the prevailing view that the Israeli occupation was for security reasons, but even with such obvious evidence I could not bring myself to abandon it.

I spent my 1983-84 sabbatical year at Jerusalem's *École Biblique* researching the Pauline Epistles. Again, the day-to-day life in Jerusalem sharpened my sensitivities. I was beginning to suspect that the Israeli occupation was not after all for security reasons, but was an expansion toward the achievement of "Greater Israel," which, I was to learn later, was the goal of even mainstream Zionism.

One incident in particular alerted me to the religious dimension of the conflict. On a spring morning in 1984, the Voice of Israel radio reported that during the night a Jewish terrorist group had been caught attempting to blow up the Dome of the Rock and the Al-Aqsa Mosque on the Haram al-Sharif (the Temple Mount), only a few hundred meters south of the *École*. Subsequently the newspapers published a picture of one of those convicted of the offence, wearing the typical dress of the religious settler movement *Gush Emunim*. He had the Book of Psalms in his hand as the judge read out the verdict. That an attempted act of such enormous international and inter-faith significance sprang from religious fervor shocked me. Settler Jews performed other acts of terror during that year, and the name of the overtly racist Rabbi Meir Kahane was seldom off the headlines.

I can date to that period also voicing my first displeasure at my perception that the land traditions of the Bible appeared to mandate the genocide of the indigenes of "Canaan." At the end of his public lecture in Tantur, I suggested to Marc Ellis, a young Jewish theologian who was developing a Jewish Theology of Liberation with strong dependence on the Hebrew prophets, that it would be no more difficult to construct a Theology of Oppression on the basis of other biblical traditions, especially those dealing with Israelite origins that demanded the destruction of other peoples.

Following my sabbatical in 1984, I returned to London where, later that year, a colleague told me of the plea of Abuna Elias Chacour of Ibillin to pilgrims from the West to meet the Christian communities, "the *Living Stones*" of the land, and not be satisfied with the "dead stones" of archaeological sites. Soon a group of interested people in London established the ecumenical trust, Living Stones, which promotes links between Christians in Britain and the Holy Land, and appointed me Chairman. In 1985 I co-led a study tour to Israel and the Occupied Territories, and led a group of priests on a "Retreat through Pilgrimage" in 1987 and made other visits in 1990 and 1991.

In 1991, I participated in an International Peace Walk from Jerusalem to Amman, and although I did not reach the destination, I gained the acquaintance of several groups of Israeli soldiers and police, enjoyed detention twice, and faced into what appeared to be an inevitable spell in prison. Officially, my crime, in the first instance, was to have trespassed into "a closed military zone" on the outskirts of Ramallah, and in the second, to have refused to leave a similarly designated area on the way from Taybeh to Jericho. The real purpose of such designations was to halt the silent walk of some 30 "peaceniks" from about 15 countries. Our presence was having a decidedly energizing effect on the Palestinians, who did not dare protest so forthrightly.

A few hours into walking silently over the Judean hills, before beginning our descent into the Jordan Valley, we were informed by the military that we were inside "a military zone." While our negotiators were engaging the Commanding Officer of the district, we sat on the side of the road and sang peace songs. I opened with a rendition, in my *bel canto* Irish-accented Hebrew, of Psalm 119 (118). My singing of this Passover song of deliverance had an obviously disturbing effect on the young soldiers "guarding" us. Formal arrest and several hours' detention in Jericho followed. To the policeman who informed me that I could make one phone call, I replied that I wished to speak to the Pope. "I am sorry, it cannot be international." My comportment during the day-long detention – insisting on the group being fed, being polite but firm under interrogation, refusing to sign my 'statement' of incrimination, etc. — left the police in no doubt about whom I considered to be the criminals.

After a long, wearying day in detention in sun-baked Jericho, we were driven to what we were assured would be a "prison." This was not good news. The principal of my college would not be pleased to read: "Sorry I cannot be there in time for class — am in prison in the Holy Land!" In the event, we were brought to a police station in Israeli-occupied East Jerusalem, and even having refused to sign another declaration, we were released. The peace-walk experience demonstrated how police, defense forces and the noble discourse of jurisprudence itself, designed to protect the vulnerable, can legitimize oppression, something I had experienced already in London while I struggled for the human rights of gypsies.

It took some time for my experiences to acquire an ideological framework. Gradually I read more of the modern history of the region. In addition to bringing a university group in 1992, I spent August in the *Ècole Biblique*, and while there interviewed prominent Palestinians, including the Latin Patriarch of Jerusalem, Michel Sabbah, the Greek Orthodox Archbishop Timotheos, the Anglican Bishop Samir Kafity, Canon Naim Ateek, and the Vice-President of Bir Zeit University, Dr. Gabi Baramki.

I made three visits in 1993, one at Easter to prepare the Cumberland Lodge Conference on Christians in the Holy Land, one for study in August, and the third to bring a group of students. Although my academic concentration in that period was on the scene of Jesus in the synagogue in Nazareth (Luke 4.16-30), my growing unease about the link between biblical spirituality and oppression stimulated me to examine the land traditions of the Bible, and so I began to read the narrative systematically with that theme in mind.

Yahweh and Ethnic Cleansing

What struck me most about the biblical narrative was that the divine promise of land was integrally linked with the mandate to exterminate the indigenous peoples, and I had to wrestle with my perception that those traditions were inherently oppressive and morally reprehensible. Even the Exodus narrative was problematic. While it portrays Yahweh as having compassion on the misery of his people, and as willing to deliver them from the Egyptians and bring them to a land flowing with milk and honey (Exodus 3:7-8), that was only part of the picture. Although the reading of Exodus 3, both in the Christian liturgy and in the classical texts of liberation theologies, halts abruptly in the middle of verse 8 at the description of the land as one "flowing with milk and honey," the biblical text itself continues, "to the country of the Canaanites, the Hittites, the Amorites, the Perizzites, the Hivites, and the Jebusites." Manifestly, the promised land, flowing with milk and honey, had no lack of indigenous peoples, and, according to the narrative, would soon flow with blood:

> When my angel goes in front of you, and brings you to the Amorites, the Hittites, the Perizzites, the Canaanites, the Hivites, and the Jebusites, and I blot them out, you shall not bow down to their gods, or worship them, or follow their practices, but you shall utterly demolish them and break their pillars in pieces (Exodus 23:23-24).

Matters got worse in the narrative of the Book of Deuteronomy. After the King of Heshbon refused passage to the Israelites, Yahweh gave him over to the Israelites who captured and utterly destroyed all the cities, killing all the men, women, and children (Deuteronomy 2:33-34). The fate of the King of Bashan was no better (3.3). Yahweh's role was central:

> When Yahweh your God brings you into the land that you are about to enter and occupy, and he clears away many nations before you — the Hittites, the Girgashites, the Amorites, the Canaanites, the Perizzites, the Hivites...and when Yahweh your God gives them over to you...you must utterly destroy them. ...Show them no mercy. ...For you are a people holy to Yahweh your God; Yahweh your God has chosen you out of all the peoples on earth to be his people, his treasured possession (Deuteronomy 7:1-11; see also 9:1-5; 11:8-9,23,31-32).

And again, from the mouth of Moses:

> But as for the towns of these peoples that Yahweh your God is giving you as an inheritance, you must not let anything that breathes remain alive. You shall annihilate them — the Hittites and the Amorites, the Canaanites and the Perizzites, the Hivites and the Jebusites — just as Yahweh your God has commanded, so that they may not teach you to do all the abhorrent things that they do for their gods, and you thus sin against Yahweh your God (Deuteronomy 20:16-18).

It was some shock to realize that the narrative presents "ethnic cleansing" as not only legitimate, but as required by the deity. The book ends with Moses's sight of the promised land before he dies (34:1-3). Although

Moses was unequaled in his deeds, he left a worthy successor, Joshua, who, after Moses had lain his hands on him, was full of the spirit of wisdom (34:4-12). So much for the preparation for entry into the Promised Land.

The first part of the Book of Joshua (chapters 2-12) describes the conquest of a few key cities, and their fate in accordance with the laws of the Holy War. Even when the Gibeonites were to be spared, the Israelite elders complained at the lapse in fidelity to the mandate to destroy all the inhabitants of the land (9:21-27). Joshua took Makkedah, utterly destroying every person in it (10:28). A similar fate befell other cities (10:29-39): everything that breathed was destroyed, as Yahweh commanded (10:40-43). Joshua utterly destroyed the inhabitants of the cities of the north as well (11:1-23). Yahweh gave to Israel all the land that he swore to their ancestors he would give them (21:43-45). The legendary achievements of Yahweh through the agencies of Moses, Aaron, and Joshua are kept before the Israelites even in their prayers: "You brought a vine out of Egypt; you drove out the nations and planted it" (Psalm 80:8; see also Psalms 78:54-55; 105:44).

By modern standards of international law and human rights, what these biblical narratives mandate are "war crimes" and "crimes against humanity." While readers might seek refuge in the claim that the problem lies with the predispositions of the modern reader, rather than with the text itself, one could not escape so easily. One must acknowledge that much of the Torah, and the Book of Deuteronomy in particular, contains menacing ideologies and racist, xenophobic and militaristic tendencies. The implications of the existence of dubious moral dispositions, presented as mandated by the divinity, within a book which is canonized as Sacred Scripture, invited the most serious investigation. Was there a way of reading the traditions which could rescue the Bible from being a blunt instrument of oppression, and acquit God of the charge of being the Great Ethnic-Cleanser?

In that August of 1994, the *École* library had just received a *Festschrift* consisting of studies in Deuteronomy. In addition to articles covering the customary source, historical-critical, and literary discussions, it contained one by F.E. Deist, with the intriguing title, "The Dangers of Deuteronomy," which discussed the role of that book in support of apartheid.[1] It dealt with the text from the perspective of its reception history, especially within the ideology of an emerging Afrikaner nationalism. During that month I also read A.G. Lamadrid's discussion of the role of the Bible and Christian theology in the Iberian conquest of Latin America.² The problem, then, went beyond academic reflection on the interpretation of ancient documents.

Somebody must have addressed the moral question before, I presumed. Back in Jerusalem in August 1995, I realized that this was not the case. Even though Gerhard von Rad lamented in 1943 that no thorough investigation of "the land" had been made, no serious study of the topic was undertaken for another 30 years. Even W.D. Davies acknowledged later that he had written his seminal work "The Gospel and the Land" at the request of friends in Jerusalem who, just before the war in 1967, had urged his support for the cause of Israel. Moreover, he confessed that he wrote both his 1982 "The Territorial Dimensions of Judaism" under the direct impact of that war, and its 1991 updated version because of the mounting need to understand the theme in the light of events in the Middle East, culminating in the Gulf War and its aftermath. I was intrigued by the frankness with which Daviespublicized his hermeneutical key: "Here I have concentrated on what in my judgment must be the beginning for an understanding of this conflict: the sympathetic attempt to comprehend the Jewish tradition."³

While Davies considers "the land" from virtually every other conceivable perspective, little attention is given to broadly moral and human rights issues. In particular, he excludes from his concern, "What happens when the understanding of the Promised Land in Judaism conflicts with the claims of the traditions and occupancy of its other peoples?" He excused himself by saying that to engage that issue would demand another volume, without indicating his intention of embarking upon such an enterprise. I wondered whether Davies would have been equally sanguine had white, Anglo-Saxon Protestants, or even white Catholics of European provenance been among the displaced people who paid the price for the prize of Zionism. Reflecting a somewhat elastic moral sense, Davies, although perturbed by the aftermath of the 1967 conquest, took the establishment of the State of Israel in his stride. Showing no concern for the foundational injustice done to the Palestinians in 1948, Davies wrote as if there were later a moral equivalence between the dispossessed Palestinians and the dispossessing Zionists. The rights of the rapist and the victim were finely balanced.

Walter Brueggemann's "The Land" brought me no further. While he saw land as perhaps "the central theme" of biblical faith, he bypassed the treatment to be meted out to the indigenous inhabitants, affirming, "What is asked is not courage to destroy enemies, but courage to keep Torah," avoiding the fact that "keeping Torah" in this context demanded accepting its xenophobic and destructive militarism. By 1994, however, Brueggemann was less sanguine, noting that while the scholastic community had provided "rich and suggestive studies on the 'land theme' in the Bible...they characteristically stop before they get to the hard part, contemporary issues of land in the Holy Land." [4]

It was beginning to dawn on me that much biblical investigation — especially that concentration on the past which is typical of the historical-critical method — was quite indifferent to moral considerations. Indeed, it was becoming clear that the discipline of biblical studies over the last hundred years reflected the Eurocentric perspectives of virtually all Western historiography and had contributed significantly to the oppression of native peoples. The benevolent interpretation of biblical traditions which advocate atrocities and war crimes had given solace to those bent on the exploitation of new lands at the expense of native peoples. While the behavior of communities and nation states is complex, and is never the result of one element of motivation, there is abundant evidence that the Bible has been, and still is for some, *the idea that redeems the conquest of the earth*. This was particularly true in the case of the Arabs of Palestine, in whose country I had reached these conclusions as I studied the Bible.

By the autumn of 1995 I was well into a book on the subject, and in November I went to discuss with Sheffield Academic Press a draft MS on "The Bible and Zionism." The editor, apprehensive at my concentration on Zionism, persuaded me to use three case studies. The task ahead, then, would require further immersion in the histories of Latin America, South Africa, and Israel, as well as a more detailed study of the biblical narrative and its interpretation in the hands of the biblical academy.

Having had my moral being sensitized by the biblical mandate to commit genocide, I was amazed that scholars had a high esteem for the Book of Deuteronomy. Indeed, commentators conventionally assess it to be a theological book *par excellence*, and the focal point of the religious history of the Old Testament. In the Nov. 14, 1995 Lattey Lecture in Cambridge University, Professor Norbert Lohfink argued that it provides a model of an utopian society in which there would be no poor.[5] In my role as the formal proposer of a vote of thanks — I was the chairperson of the Catholic Biblical Association of Great Britain - I invited him to consider whether, in the light of that book's insistence on a mandate to commit genocide, the utopian society would be possible only after the invading Israelites had wiped out the indigenous inhabitants. The protocol of the Lattey Lecture left the last word with me, and subsequently I was given a second word, being invited to deliver the 1997 Lattey Lecture, for which I chose the title, "A Land flowing with Milk, Honey, and People."[6]

O Little Bantustan of Bethlehem

The final revision of my study on the relation between the Bible and colonialism was undertaken in 1996-97 while I was Visiting Professor in Bethlehem University and Scholar-in-Residence in Tantur Ecumenical Institute, Jerusalem. My context was a persistent reminder of the degradation and oppression which colonizing enterprises inflict on their indigenes. I also became more aware of the collusion of Western scholarship in the enterprise.

Working against a background of bullet fire, and in the shadow of tanks, added a certain intensity to my research. Several bullets landed on the flat roof of Tantur on 25-26 September 1996. Two Palestinians, one a graduate of the University, were killed in Bethlehem, and many more, Palestinians and Israeli soldiers, were killed in the disturbances elsewhere in the West Bank. However, with no bullets flying in Jerusalem on the 26th, I was able to deliver my advertised public lecture in the Swedish Christian Study Center, entitled "Does the God of the Bible sanction Ethnic Cleansing?" By mid-December I was able to send the MS of "The Bible and Colonialism" to Sheffield Academic Press.

I preached at the 1996 Christmas Midnight Mass in Bethlehem University, presided over by Msgr. Montezemolo, the Holy See's Apostolic Delegate, a key player in the signing of the Fundamental Agreement between the Holy See and the State of Israel on 30 December 1993. I reflected with the congregation that, notwithstanding the Christmas rhetoric about God's Glory in the Highest Heaven and Peace on Earth, the reality of Bethlehem brought one down to earth rather quickly. I assured them that passing by the checkpoint between Bethlehem and Jerusalem twice a day made me boil with anger at the humiliation which the colonizing enterprise of Zionism had inflicted on the people of the region. I suggested that the Christmas narratives portray the ordinary people as the heroes and the rulers as the anti-heroes, as if assuring believers that the mighty will be cast down, and that God is working for the oppressed today. I would meet His Excellency again soon.

On 30 December, I listened to Msgr. Montezemolo lecture in Notre Dame on the third anniversary of the Fundamental Agreement between the Holy See and Israel. The audience was composed exclusively of expatriate Christians and Israeli Jews, with not a Palestinian in sight.

Well into the question time, I violated the somewhat sycophantic atmosphere: "I had expected that the Agreement would have given the Holy See some leverage in putting pressure on Israel *vis-à-vis* the Palestinians, if only on the matter of freedom to worship in Jerusalem — Palestinians have been forbidden entry into even East Jerusalem, whether on Friday or Sunday, since March 1993."

His Excellency replied rhetorically, "Do you not think that the Holy See is doing all it can?" At the reception afterwards, a certain Ambassador Gilboa, one of the Israeli architects of the Agreement, berated me in a most aggressive fashion for my question. Rather than assuming the posture of a culprit, I took the attack to him on the matter of the Jews having "kicked out" the Palestinians in 1948. "No, they were not kicked out," he, who was a soldier at the time, insisted. "In fact helicopters dropped leaflets on the Arab towns, beseeching the inhabitants to stay put, etc."

I told him I did not believe him, and cited even the Israeli revisionist historiographer, Benny Morris, whom he dismissed as a compulsive attention-seeker. It was obvious all round the room that a not insignificant altercation was taking place. In the hope of discouraging him from trying to stifle the truth in the future, I assured him that he should have remained a soldier, because he had the manners of a "corner-boy," and not what I expected from a diplomat. I went home righteous.

Academic life rolled on. My 28 Feb. 1997 lecture on "The Bible and Zionism" seemed to perplex several of the students of Bethlehem Bible College. Most of the questions reflected a literalist understanding of the Bible, and I struggled to convey the impression that there were forms of discourse other than history.

Having visited the Christian Peacemaker Team in Hebron as a gesture of solidarity on 6 March, I returned home for the Tantur public lecture on "The Future of Religious Zionism" by the Jewish philosopher, Professor David Hartman. It was an eventful occasion. Hartman gave a dazzling exegesis on the theme of covenant, from the Bible through the Rabbis, to Zionism. My journal takes the matter up from the second half of his talk, devoted to questions.

I made the fourth intervention, to the effect that in being brought through the stages of understanding of the covenant, from the Bible to Rabbinic Judaism, I was enchanted, and much appreciative. However, I was shocked to hear Zionism described as "the high point of covenantal spirituality." Zionism, as I saw it, both in its rhetoric and in its practice, was not an ideology of sharing, but one of displacing. I was shocked, therefore, that what others might see as an example of 19th-century colonial plunder was being clothed in the garment of spirituality.

Somewhat shaken, Professor Hartman thanked me for my question, and set about putting the historical record straight. The real problem was that the Arabs had not welcomed Jews back to their homeland. Moreover, the displacement of the Arabs was never intended, but was forced on the Zionist leadership by the attack of the Arab armies in 1948. Nevertheless, great developments in history sometimes require initial destruction: consider how the USA had defeated totalitarianism, although this was preceded by the displacement of the Indians.

On the following day, in the discussion time after my final session of teaching on "Jesus the Liberator" in Tantur, one of the Continuing Education students brought the discussion back to the previous day's deliberations. He was very embarrassed by my attack on "that holy man."

There was a particularly lively exchange with several getting into the discussion. A second student said that he was delighted with my question yesterday and was sure that it represented the disquiet of many of the group. A third responded enthusiastically to my liberation ethic, saying that it disturbed him, but he had to cope with the disturbance. An American priest came to me afterwards, saying how much he appreciated my courage in speaking yesterday, and on a previous occasion, etc. His enthusiasm was not shared by everyone. After the class, an advertising notice appeared on the board from the overseer of the Scholar's Colloquium. It read, "Dr. Michael Prior presents a largish paper, 'Zionism: from the Secular to the Sacred,' which is a chapter from a book he is in the process of writing." The next paragraph read:

> Zionism is a subject on which there are hot opinions — not least from the author himself. Some have suggested to me that this disunity is a reason why we should not discuss such matters at all. I believe the opposite: the quality of hot opinions is best tested in a scholarly discussion, where they must be supported by evidence and good argument. One can even learn something. Welcome!

The Swedish New Testament scholar, Bengt Holmberg, chaired the Colloquium. The first scholar to respond to my paper, a U.S. Catholic veteran of the Jewish-Christian dialogue, did so in a decidedly aggressive manner, accusing me of disloyalty to the Church, etc.

The second was long in praise.

The third intimated that there was nothing new in the paper, and rambled on about the Zionists' intentions to bring benefits to the indigenous population, etc. Losing patience, I asked him to produce evidence for his claims, adding that not only was there not such evidence, but the evidence there showed that the Zionist ideologues were virtually at one in their determination to rid the land of Arabs.

A fourth scholar, a Dutch Protestant veteran of the Jewish-Christian dialogue, chastised me for my audacity in addressing the question at all, insisting that I should be silent, because I was an outsider and a Christian.

I rose to the challenge. Was I understanding him to say that, having seen the distress of the Palestinian people for myself, I should now not comment on it? Was he asking me to deny my experience, or merely to mute my critique? I assured the Colloquium that as a biblical scholar, and an ongoing witness to what transpired in the region, I considered it an obligation to protest what was going on. Once again, the admiring remarks were made later, in private.

The proofs of "The Bible and Colonialism" arrived on Good Friday. I got my first taste of teargas in the vicinity of Rachel's Tomb on my way to Easter Sunday Mass at St. Catherine's in Bethlehem. On 3 April, I delivered the Tantur public lecture, "The Moral Problem of the Bible's Land Traditions,"' followed by questions, both appreciative and hostile. Uniquely for the series, the lecture was not advertised in the Jerusalem Post. In dealing with a trilogy of hostile questions I availed of the opportunity to say that I considered Zionism to be one of the most pernicious ideologies of the 20th century, particularly evil because of its essential link with religious values.

Stars from the West studded the sky over Bethlehem for the celebrations of Tantur's 25th birthday (25-28 May 1997). Under the light of the plainly visible Hale-Bopp comet, a frail Teddy Kollek was introduced at the opening ceremony as though he were the founder of the Institute. A choir from the USA sang, one song in Hebrew. Palestinian faces, not least that of Afif Safieh, the Palestinian Delegate to the UK and the Holy

See, looked decidedly out of joint throughout the opening festivities. But the Palestinians were not altogether forgotten, being thanked profusely for their work in the kitchen and around the grounds.

Moreover, for the lecture on "Christians of the Holy Land" which was given on May 27, prominent Palestinians were invited to speak from the floor. Although the lecture was billed to be presented by a distinguished expatriate scholar "with local presenters," in fact the Palestinian savants had been invited only to the audience floor. Having excused himself from dealing with the political context, the lecturer delivered an urbane, accomplished historical perspective.

The token Palestinians were invited to speak from the floor, first Naim Ateek, then Mitri Raheb, and then Kevork Hintlian. After two rabbis had their say, also from the floor, I was allowed to speak, wishing to make two points: that my experience with the Palestinians had impressed upon me their unity, rather than their diversity, and, secondly, that the Jewish-Christian dialogue had been hijacked by a Zionist agenda. After one more sentence had escaped from my mouth the Chair stopped me short. I had broken the Solemn Silence. This was the third time that year I had been prevented from speaking in public. I paused, producing a most uncomfortable silence, thanked him, and sat down.

Saturday 31 May, 1997 being the 28th anniversary of my ordination, I determined to do something different. Since it was also the Feast of the Visitation, I decided that I would go to Ein Karem, the traditional site of Mary's visit to her cousin Elizabeth. But on the way, I would call at Jabal Abu Ghneim, the hill opposite Tantur, which, despite UN condemnation, was being prepared for an Israeli settlement. The teeth of the high-tech machinery had cut into the rock, having chewed up thousands of trees. Joseph Conrad's phrase, "the relentless progress of our race," kept coming at me.

On the way to Ein Karem, I visited Mount Herzl to see the grave of the founder of Zionism. Knowing that I would also visit the grave of Yitzhak Rabin, I was struck by the irony of the situation. Theodor Herzl was sure that Jews could survive only in their own nation state. Nevertheless, he died a natural death in Europe, and was re-interred in the new state in 1949, while Prime Minister Rabin, born in Palestine, was gunned down by a Jewish religious zealot in what was intended to be the sole haven for Jews.

Back in England

I returned to London in July 1997. By December, "The Bible and Colonialism" and "Western Scholarship and the History of Palestine" were hot off the press. In "The Bible and Colonialism" I promised that I would discuss elsewhere the more theological aspects of Zionism, and, while still in Jerusalem in 1997, I had laid out my plans for writing the book I had really wanted to write some years earlier.

I submitted a draft MS to a distinguished publisher in November 1997, and even though the anonymous reader found it to be "a brilliant book which must be published," the press declined, because, I was informed orally, the press had "a very strong Jewish list," and could not offend its Jewish contributors and readers. While an American publishing company judged it to be "a prodigious achievement of historical and theological investigation" and "a very important work," it deemed that it would not really suit its publishing program. Routledge "bit the bullet," publishing it under the title "Zionism and the State of Israel: A Moral Inquiry."[7]

On the basis of his having read my "The Bible and Colonialism," Professor Heikki Räisänen of the University of Helsinki invited me to address the most prestigious of the international biblical conferences, the Society of Biblical Literature International Conference (Helsinki-Lahti, 16-22 July 1999) on the subject, "The Bible and Zionism." The session at which I was invited to speak dealt with "'Reception History and Moral Criticism of the Bible," and I was preceded by Professors Robert Jewett (USA) and David Clines (UK) on aspects of Paul and Job, respectively.

When my hour came, I invited biblical scholarship not to maintain an academic detachment from significant engagement in contemporary issues. I noted that "the view that the Bible provides the title-deed for the establishment of the State of Israel and for its policies since 1948 is so pervasive even within mainstream Christian theology and university biblical studies, that the very attempt to raise the issue is sure to elicit opposition. The disfavor usually took the form of personal abuse, and the intimidation of publishers."

In the light of what happened next I might have added that one is seldom honored by having the substantive issues addressed in the usual way.

After I had delivered my 25-minute lecture the official respondent, who had my paper a month in advance, said he would bypass the usual niceties ("A very fine paper, etc."), and got down to his objections, which were so standard as not to deserve my refutation. Instead I suggested to the Chair to open up the discussion.

Some five Israelis in turn took up the challenge. "Jews have always longed for the land." "They never intended displacing anyone." "The land was empty — almost." "I was wrong historically: Herzl never intended dislocating the Arabs."

I interrupted, quoting Herzl's 12 June 1895 diary entry — in the original German for good measure — about his endeavor to expel the poor population, etc.

I was berated for having raised a "political matter" in an academic conference: "See what can happen when one abandons the historical critical method!" Another Israeli professor began by saying, "I am very pleased to have been here this morning," but added, "because I understand better now how anti-Semitism can present itself as anti-Zionism, all under the guise of academic scholarship." A cabal, including at least one Israeli and a well-known scholar from Germany, clapped. The Chair had to restore order.

In the course of my "defense" I reiterated that it was the displacement of another people that raised the moral problematic for me. I had witnessed the effects of the oppression rather more than even most of the audience. Having been given the last word, I professed that until Israelis acknowledge their having displaced another people and make some reparation and accommodation, there would be no future for the state.

In the course of the following day several who had attended expressed their appreciation, albeit in private. A Finnish scholar congratulated me on having raised a vital issue, adding, "The way you were received added sharpness to your argument." A distinguished biblical scholar from Germany, who was very distressed by my having raised the question, later pleaded that his people were responsible for killing six million Jews.

The Importance of the Issue

I have learned that, distinctively in the case of Zionist colonization, a determined effort was made to rid the terrain altogether of the native population, since their presence in any number would frustrate the grand design of establishing a Jewish state. The necessity of removing the Arabs was recognized from the beginning of the Zionist enterprise

— and advocated by all major Zionist ideologues from Theodor Herzl to Ehud Barak — and was meticulously planned and executed in 1948 and 1967. In their determination to present an unblemished record of the Zionist achievement, the fabricators of propagandistic Zionist history are among the most accomplished practitioners of the strange craft of source-doctoring, rewriting not only their history, but the documents upon which such a history was based. The propagandistic intent was to hide things said and done, and to bequeath to posterity only a sanitized version of the past.

In any case, the argument for the compelling need of Jews to settle in a Jewish state does not constitute a right to displace an indigenous population. And even if it had never been intended from the start, which it most certainly was, the moral problematic arises most acutely precisely from the fact that Zionism has wreaked havoc on the indigenous population, and not a little inconvenience on several surrounding states. Nor can the *Shoah* (Holocaust) be appealed to credibly justify the destruction of an innocent third party. It is a dubious moral principle to regard the barbaric treatment of Jews by the Third Reich as constituting a right to establish a Jewish state at the expense of an innocent third party. Surely the victims of Auschwitz would not have approved.

My study of the Bible in the Land of the Bible brought me face to face with the turbulence of Israel-Palestine and raised questions not only about the link between biblical interpretation and colonial exploitation but about the nature of the biblical narrative itself. An academic interest became a consuming moral imperative.

Why should the State of Israel, any more than any other state, be such a challenge to morality? The first reason, I suggest, derives from the general moral question attendant upon the forcible displacement of an indigenous people from its homeland. The second springs from the unique place that the land has in the Sacred Scriptures of both Jews and Christians, and the significance attached to it as the location of the state for Jews. In addition, there is the positive assessment of the State of Israel on the part of the majority of religious Jews of various categories, as well as in certain Christian ecclesial and theological circles.

As a biblical scholar, I have been shocked to discover that the only plausible validation for the displacement of the Palestinians derived from a naïve interpretation of the Bible, and that in many Church and academic parties — and not only the "fundamentalist" wing — biblical literalism swept away any concerns deriving from considerations of morality. I contend that fidelity to the literary genre of the biblical traditions and respect for the evidence provided mainly by archaeological investigation demands a rejection of such simplistic readings of the biblical narratives of land, and of the prophetic oracles of restoration.

And to these academic perspectives, one must add one of faith, namely, that God is fundamentally moral, and, for those espousing the Christian vision, loves all his people, irrespective of race, etc.

Rather than relate the establishment of the State of Israel to the *Shoah*, I have been led gradually to situate Zionism within the category of xenophobic imperialism, so characteristic of the major European powers towards the end of the 19th century. I consider the espousal of it by a majority of Jews world-wide to mark the nadir of Jewish morality. Because I trust in a God before whom tyranny ultimately dissolves, and because one learns something from history, I have no doubt that a future generation of diaspora and Israeli Jews will repudiate its presumptions, and repent for the injustices perpetrated on the Palestinians by their fathers and grandfathers.

While I regret the descent of Judaism into the embrace of Zionism, there is little I can do about it. However, the degree to which a thoroughly Zionised Judaism infects the so-called Jewish-Christian dialogue — which I prefer to designate "a monologue in two voices" — is a matter of grave concern. I am perturbed that concurrence with a Zionist reading of Jewish history — that Jews everywhere, and at all times, wanted to re-establish a nation state in Palestine (with no concern for the indigenous population), etc.— is virtually a component of the credo of the dialogue. In that fabricated scenario, the planned, and systematically executed dislocation of the Palestinian population, far from incurring the wrath of post-colonial liberalism, becomes an object of honor, and even religious significance. While most Jews world-wide — there are notable exceptions — allow themselves to be deluded by such perspectives, I see no reason why Christians should.

God the Ethnic Cleanser?

Often I am asked: How do you as a Catholic priest and biblical scholar explain to an ordinary believer the Yahweh-sanctioned ethnic-cleansing mandated in some of the narrative of the Old Testament? Is not this also the Word of God? Such questions have forced themselves on me in a particular way as a result of my contact with the Holy Land. Let me indicate some of my perspectives. But first, let us look at the stakes.

Recently a full-page advertisement in the 10 September 2000 New York Times, signed by over 150 Jewish scholars and leaders, stated:

> Christians can respect the claim of the Jewish people upon the land of Israel. The most important event for Jews since the Holocaust has been the reestablishment of a Jewish state in the Promised Land. As members of a biblically-based religion, Christians appreciate that Israel was promised — and given — to Jews as the physical center of the covenant between them and God. Many Christians support the State of Israel for reasons far more profound than mere politics. As Jews, we applaud this support.

Here we see clothed in the garment of piety the Zionist enterprise, which was determined to create a state for Jews at the expense of the indigenous Arab people — a product of the nationalistic and imperialistic spirit of 19th-century Europe.

Whatever pangs of conscience one might have about the expulsion of a million Palestinian Arabs, and the destruction of their villages to ensure they would not return, the Bible can salve it. Zionism, a program originally despised by both wings of Judaism, Orthodox and Reform, as being anti-religious (by the Orthodox) and contrary to the universal mission of Judaism (by Reform Jewry), is now at the core of the Jewish *credo*. And credulous Christians allow themselves to be sucked into the vortex. Only when Zionism is being evaluated are normal rules of morality suspended; only here is ethnic-cleansing applauded by the religious spirit.

Many theologians on seeing how the revered sacred text has been used as an instrument of oppression seek refuge in the view that it is the misuse of the Bible, rather than the text itself which is the problem. The blame is shifted from the non-problematic biblical text to the perverse predispositions of the interpreter.

This "solution" evades the problem. It must be acknowledged that several traditions within the Bible lend themselves to oppressive interpretations and applications, precisely because of their inherently oppressive nature.

Towards a Moral Reading of the Bible

My approach is set forth in a chapter of my book, "The Bible and Colonialism. A Moral Critique."[8] I begin by stressing how important it is to acknowledge the existence of texts of unsurpassed violence within Sacred Scripture, and to recognize them to be an affront to moral sensitivities. The problem is not only theoretical. In addition to being morally reprehensible texts, some have fueled terrible injustices through colonialist enterprises.

The Holy War traditions of the Old Testament pose an especially difficult moral problem. In addition to portraying God as one who cherishes the slaughter of his created ones, they acquit the killer of moral responsibility for his destruction, presenting it as a religious obligation.

Every effort must be made to rescue the Bible from being a blunt instrument in the oppression of one people by another. If a naïve interpretation leads to such unacceptable conclusions, what kind of exegesis can rescue it?

Some exegetes note that Christians read the Old Testament in the light of the life and paschal mystery of Christ. In such a perspective, the writings of the Old Testament contain certain "imperfect and provisional" elements, which the divine pedagogy could not eliminate right away. The Bible, then, reflects a considerable moral development, which finds its completion in the New Testament. I do not find this proposal satisfactory.

The attempts of the Fathers of the Church to eliminate the scandal caused by particular texts of the Bible do little for me. The allegorical presentation of Joshua leading the people into the land of Canaan as a type of Christ, who leads Christians into the true promised land does not impress.

The Catholic Church deals with the embarrassment of having divinely mandated ethnic cleansing in the biblical narrative by either excluding it altogether from public use, or excising the most offensive verses. The disjuncture between this censoring of the Word of God and the insistence on the divine provenance of the whole of the Scriptures has not been satisfactorily resolved.

There is another method which is more amenable to modern sensibilities, one which takes seriously the literary forms of the materials, the circumstances of their composition, and relevant non-literary evidence. According to this view, the fundamental tenet of the Protestant Reformation that the Bible can be understood in a straightforward way must be abandoned. Narratives purporting to describe the past are not necessarily accurate records of it. One must respect the distinctive literary forms within the biblical narrative — legend, fabricated myths of the past, prophecy and apocalyptic, etc.

The relevant biblical narratives of the past are not simple history, but reflect the religious and political ideologies of their much later authors. It is now part of the scholarly consensus that the patriarchal narratives of Genesis do not record events of an alleged patriarchal period, but are retrojections into a past about which the writers knew little, reflecting the author's intentions at the later period of composition. It is naïve, then, to cleave to the view that God made the promise of progeny and land to Abraham after the fashion indicated in Genesis 15.

The Exodus narrative poses particular difficulties for any reader who is neither naïve nor amoral. It is the entrance (*Eisodus*) into the land of milk and honey which keeps the hope of the wandering Israelites alive. It is high time that readers read the narrative with sensitivity to the innocent third-party about to be exterminated, that is, "with the eyes of the Canaanites."

Moreover, there is virtual unanimity among scholars that the model of tribal conquest as narrated in Joshua 1-12 is unsustainable. Leaving aside the witness of the Bible, we have no evidence that there was a Hebrew conquest. Evidence from archaeology, extra-biblical literature, etc., points in an altogether different direction from that propounded by Joshua 1-12. It suggests a sequence of periods marked by a gradual and peaceful coalescence of disparate peoples into a group of highland dwellers whose achievement of a new sense of unity culminated only with the entry of the Assyrian administration. The Iron Age settlements on the central hills of Palestine, from which the later kingdom of Israel developed, reflect continuity with Canaanite culture, and repudiate any ethnic distinction between "Canaanites" and "Israelites." Israel's origins, then, were within Canaan, not outside it. There was neither invasion from outside, nor revolution within.

A historiography of Israelite origins based solely, or primarily on the biblical narratives is an artificial construct influenced by certain religious motivations obtaining at a time long post-dating any verifiable evidence of events. Accordingly, *pace* the 150 plus Jewish scholars and rabbis who signed The New York Times ad, the biblical narrative is not sufficient to transform barbarism into piety.

Conclusion

Western theological scholarship, while strong in its critique of repressive regimes elsewhere, gives a wide berth to Zionism. Indeed a moral critique of its impact on the Palestinians is ruled out.

I try to break the silence in my "The Bible and Colonialism" and "Zionism and the State of Israel." The former explores the moral question of the impact which colonialist enterprises, fueled by the biblical paradigm, have had on the indigenous populations in general, while the latter deals with the impact of Zionism on the Palestinians. They are explorations into terrain virtually devoid of inquirers, which attempt to map out some of the contours of that terrain. They subject the land traditions of the Bible to an evaluation which derives from general ethical principles and criteria of human decency, such as are enshrined in conventions of human rights and international law.

Such an enterprise is necessary. When people are dispossessed, dispersed and humiliated, not only with alleged divine support, but at the alleged express command of God, one's moral self recoils in horror. Any association of God with the destruction of people must be subjected to an ethical analysis. The obvious contradiction between what some claim to be God's will and ordinary civilized, decent behavior poses the question as to whether God is a chauvinistic, nationalistic and militaristic xenophobe. It also poses the problem of biblical prophecy finding its fulfillment in what even unbelievers would regard as a form of "ethnic cleansing."

I consider that biblical studies and theology should deal with the real conditions of people's lives, and not satisfy themselves with comfortable survival in an academic or ecclesial ghetto. I am concerned about the use of the Bible as a legitimization for colonialism and its consequences. My academic work addresses aspects of biblical hermeneutics, and informs a wider public on issues which have implications for human well-being, as well as for allegiance to God.

While such a venture might be regarded as an instructive academic contribution by any competent scholar, to assume responsibility for doing so is for me, who has witnessed the dispossession, dispersion and humiliation of the Palestinians, of the order of a moral imperative. It is high time that biblical scholars, church people, and Western intellectuals read the biblical narratives of the promise of land "with the eyes of the Canaanites."[9]

End Notes

1. Deist, F. E., The Dangers of Deuteronomy: A Page from the Reception History of the Book, in Martinez, F. Garcia, A. Hilhorst, J.T.A.G.M. van Ruiten, and A.S. van der Woud (eds), "Studies in Deuteronomy. In Honor of C.J. Labuschagne on the Occasion of his 65th Birthday," 1994, Leiden/New York/Köln: Brill, 13-29.

2. Lamadrid, A.G., Canaán y América. La Biblia y la Teologia medieval ante la Conquista de la Tierra, in "Escritos de Biblia y Oriente. Bibliotheca Salmanticensis," Estudios 38, 1981, Salamanca-Jerusalén: Universidad Pontificia, 329-46.

3. Davies, W.D., "The Gospel and the Land. Early Christianity and Jewish Territorial Doctrine," 1974, Berkeley: University of California Press. See also his "The Territorial Dimensions of Judaism," 1982, Berkeley: University of California Press; and his "The Territorial Dimensions of Judaism. With a Symposium and Further Reflections," 1991, Minneapolis: Fortress.

4. Brueggemann, Walter, "The Land. Place as Gift, and Challenge in Biblical Faith," 1977, Philadelphia: Fortress. See also his Forward in March, W. Eugene, "Israel and the Politics of Land. A Theological Case Study," 1994, Louisville: Westminster/John Knox Press.

5. Lohfink, Norbert, The Laws of Deuteronomy. Project for a World without any Poor, in Scripture Bulletin, 1996, 26:2-19.

6. Prior, Michael, "A Land flowing with Milk, Honey, and People," 1997, Cambridge: Von Hügel Institute; and in Scripture Bulletin, 28 (1998):2-17.

7. Prior, Michael, "Zionism and the State of Israel: A Moral Inquiry," 1999, London and New York: Routledge.

8. Prior, Michael, "The Bible and Colonialism. A Moral Critique," 1997, Sheffield: Sheffield Academic Press.

9. My study of the Bible in the Land of the Bible obviously aided me in seeing "with the eyes of the Canaanites." Others, surely, have had no less interesting experiences to tell, some of which I have collected in "They Came and They Saw. Western Christian Experiences of the Holy Land," Michael Prior, ed., 2000, London: Melisende.

Israel's Anti-Civilian Weapons
John Mahoney

[**Editor's note**: The prophet Ezekiel did his work both before and after the Babylonian destruction of Judah and Jerusalem in 587 B.C. In chs. 1-24, he spoke to a people that was refusing to learn from the events of 597 B.C., and in chs. 33-48 he spoke words of hope to a people devastated by the catastrophic events of 587 B.C. Among other things, he told them how they were to treat the non-Israelites with whom they would share the land after their return from exile in Babylon. He wrote:

> You shall divide this land among you according to the tribes of Israel. You shall allot it as an inheritance for yourselves and for the *aliens* who reside among you and have begotten children among you. They shall be as citizens of Israel; with you they shall be allotted an inheritance among the tribes of Israel. In whatever tribe *aliens* reside, there you shall assign them their inheritance, says the Lord God. (47:21-23)

In what follows, John Mahoney describes how the Palestinians are being treated by those who have robbed them of their homeland.]

Israel's Anti-Civilian Bullets

Some Israelis liken them to prophylactics that leak. Others to hoods that mask sinister cores. Avigdor Feldman, an Israeli lawyer, calls them rubber stamps for the deployment of excessive violence against a civilian population.[1]

In 1999 the Israeli army, anticipating the recent civilian uprising in the occupied West Bank and Gaza, trained four battalions of soldiers for low-intensity conflict. One of them, dubbed Nahshon, specializes in urban warfare. Its troops train in mock Palestinian villages constructed in two Israeli Defense Forces (IDF) bases. According to an article in *The Jerusalem Post* of 27 October 2000, these specially trained Israeli units aim to hit their targets in a way that will cripple them, while keeping the death statistics low.

Why cripple and not kill? Israeli Prime Minister Ehud Barak gave the reason in *The Jerusalem Post* of 30 October 2000: "Were there not 140 Palestinian casualties at this point, but rather 400 or 1,000, this ... would perhaps damage Israel a great deal."

What the prime minister means is that, in the dry statistics of headline news, those injured do not count. *The Jerusalem Post* writer speculates about these faceless, often nameless Palestinians: "Who will pay attention to their fate after the injury, in overcrowded and under-equipped hospitals? Who will stop to think how many of them will die slowly, from their wounds, or remain disabled, blind or maimed for life? Or to think about their chances to survive the siege and starvation inflicted on their people?"

In the six years of the first intifada (1987-1993), Israelis wounded 18,000 Palestinians. In the first month of the new intifada (October 2000), Israelis shot at and injured over 7,000 Palestinians, most of them stone-throwing demonstrators, many of these young children under 14 years of age.[2]

Listen to Sgt. Raz, a 20-year-old sharpshooter from the Nahshon battalion, quoted in the October 27th *Jerusalem Post*: "I shot two people … in their knees. It's supposed to break their bones and neutralize them but not kill them. How did I feel? Well actually, I felt pretty satisfied with myself. I felt I could do what I was trained to do."

What Sgt. Raz was shooting was a rubber-coated metal bullet. What he didn't say, however, but what *The Jerusalem Post* article goes on to report, is that Israeli sharpshooters play a little game among themselves, one that tests how really good they are: they aim for an eye.

Often enough, they succeed. Reports of eye injuries come in daily. According to a 19 October 2000 report from the Palestinian human rights organization LAW, "On October 11, Mizan Diagnostic Hospital in Hebron reported treating 11 Palestinians for eye injuries, including three children. El Nasir Ophthalmic Hospital in Gaza has treated 16 people for eye injuries, including 13 children. Nine of them lost one of their eyes." And a LAW report of 2 November 2000 adds that from 29 September to 25 October, Jerusalem's St. John's Eye Hospital has treated 50 patients for eye injuries.

What must it feel like to place a child's eye in the crosshairs of your rifle? Does it ease a soldier's conscience if his or her bullets are rubber-coated?

It shouldn't. The fact is, rubber-coated projectiles can do more bodily damage than conventional live fire.

The Palestine Red Crescent Society has recovered four types of bullets of various caliber used by the Israeli army against Palestinians: black cylinder, or rubber-coated steel (or metal) bullets; black ball, or thin plastic-coated steel balls; yellow, or solid rubber balls; and non-coated steel balls. These last bullets are larger than what the soldiers generally use for live ammunition and for that reason affect a wider surface area, damaging more muscles and organs, and actually causing a number of fatalities.[3]

It is, however, the rubber-coated steel bullets specifically that, according to the Israeli human rights organization B'Tselem, cause most of the blinding, broken bones, severe internal organ damage, and trauma.

In 1998, B'Tselem found that, from January 1988 to the end of November 1998, at least 58 Palestinians were killed by rubber-coated steel bullets, including 28 children under 17-years-of age, of whom 13 were under the age of 13. Dr. Robert Kirschner, a forensic scientist working for the Boston-based Physicians for Human Rights, gave the following forensic opinion of "rubber bullets" for the B'Tselem report:

> The tissue damage caused by a rubber-coated steel ball perforating the skin is much greater than that caused by a normal bullet, which pierces the skin more easily because of its more aerodynamic shape and smaller diameter. The wounds are more akin to severe blunt trauma injury, and cylindrical rubber bullets cause even greater damage as they are tumbling when they strike the body. There is a greater tearing, or lacerating, effect, often gaping holes, and more internal damage along the path of these projectiles. Although they rarely penetrate deeply as their kinetic energy is dissipated in the superficial tissues, only a few cm of penetration is necessary to enter the brain, thoracic and abdominal cavities, heart, lungs, liver, gastrointestinal tract, or spinal column. Rubber bullet injuries to the spinal cord have produced paraplegia and quadriplegia. While penetrating injuries, particularly to the head, are more likely to be fatal, three of the ten fatalities reported by Hiss et al in their autopsy series were of blunt trauma injuries to the head or neck with internal injuries caused by transmission of kinetic energy into deeper tissues.[4]

The B'Tselem report goes on to note that children and the elderly are at greater risk of serious injury or death from rubber-coated steel bullets because of their more fragile bone structure and smaller muscle mass.

And small children, due to their size, are more susceptible to being hit in the upper body either directly or by rubber bullets ricocheting off the ground.

How bad are these rubber-coated steel bullets? Bad enough that the U.S. Department of State has criticized the Israeli government for their use and misuse. The 1998 Report on Human Rights Practices states:

> Israeli soldiers and police sometimes used live ammunition or rubber-coated metal bullets, which can be lethal, in situations other than when their lives were in danger and sometimes shot suspects in the upper body and head. During the year, Israeli soldiers shot in the head and killed, with rubber-coated metal bullets, three Palestinians under the age of 18.

Because they are the targets, Palestinian youngsters have become authorities of sort on rubber-coated steel bullets. They collect them much like American kids collect baseball cards. And they've learned how to discern what's coming at them. They need only to check the type of canister on the end of the high-velocity rifles pointed at them to know which bullets are being used. If the canister is about 10 inches long, an inch wide, and looks like a very long silencer, the gun is shooting plastic-coated steel balls that are 95% by weight metal, 1.8 cm in diameter, and surrounded by a one mm coating of plastic. Palestinians know they can cause extensive damage such as broken bones, tissue and organ damage, and death. Because of the large number of brain injuries caused by this type of bullet, some doctors have devised a new surgical tool, a long slender magnet, used to pull the bullet out through the entry pathway.[5]

If, however, the canister is about the size of a 12-ounce can of soda, the gun is shooting rubber-coated steel bullets which, being 74% by weight metal, are more accurately called, according to the Reuters news agency, "rubber coated metal bullets with the rubber slashed to release the metal in the body of the victim." These bullets can cause severe bruises, tissue and organ damage, eye loss, broken bones, and death.[6] The soda can at the end of an Israeli rifle is, for Palestinians, far from the pause that refreshes.

In November 2000, Physicians for Human Rights issued a report of its independent inquiry into the most recent killings of Palestinians. An examination of hundreds of Palestinian casualties found that scores had been killed or badly injured by rubber-coated steel bullets fired, "excessively and inappropriately," contrary to army rules, at close range. The soldiers, the report concluded, "appeared to be shooting to inflict harm, rather than solely in self-defense."

None of which would come as news to Palestinians. There is, however, one weapon in Israel's anti-civilian arsenal that is new. According to a *London Times* report of 17 October 2000, stone-throwing youths in Ramallah watched, stunned, as men and boys at the barricades collapsed with small bullet holes in their chests, testicles, arms and hips. Tamir Barghouti, nephew of Marwan Barghouti, leader of the West Bank intifada, was one such casualty.

Palestinians are used to the rubber-coated steel bullets in their daily ritual of ducking and diving and hurling stones. But bullets that come out of nowhere terrify them. There are no bangs, no smoking guns. Victims just collapse and bleed, sometimes unnoticed. "I didn't hear a thing. I didn't feel much. I just fell over," recalled Tahir Afaneh, 18, speaking from a bed in Ramallah's central hospital, where he was being treated for a bullet lodged in his pelvis. Hosni Atari, the doctor who was treating him, said he had never seen the results of the new Israeli weapon before. Hollow-nosed bullets open up like umbrellas on impact, spin about, then chew up internal organs; seldom do they leave an exit wound. That day alone Dr. Atari had treated seven patients hit by the "new" weapon.[7]

It is, in fact, an old weapon. Called dumdum bullets by the British, after the munitions factory at Dumdum, India, where they were first manufactured in the late 19th century, they are designed to inflict maximum damage. So vicious are they, the 1899 Hague Conference adopted the Hague Declaration IV (3) by which the parties agreed to "abstain from the use of bullets which expand or flatten easily in the human body, such as bullets with a hard envelope which does not entirely cover the core or is pierced with incisions."

Israel denies using dumdum bullets. Dr. Hosni Atari and Tahir Afaneh know otherwise.

Israel's Anti-Civilian Toxins

That 750,000 Palestinians were expelled from over 400 towns and villages in 1948 is now well documented. Less well known is how Zionists made sure these Palestinians never returned home: they poisoned their wells with typhus and dysentery bacteria.

Bacteriological agents also were used in the assault on the coastal town of Acre. Because of its natural defenses, the Zionist forces could not overrun Acre as easily as they did other villages. So they put bacteria into a spring that fed the town. The spring, called Capri, ran from the north near a Jewish farming collective. Once the people of Acre began to get sick, Jewish forces occupied the town.

This worked so well in Acre that the Zionists sent a Haganah division dressed as Arabs into Gaza, where Egyptian forces were positioned. The Egyptians, however, caught them in the act of putting two cans of bacteria, typhus and dysentery, into the civilian water supply. One of the captured saboteurs was quoted as saying, "In war, there is no sentiment."

How do we know all this? From the Hebrew press. In an article published 13 August 1993 in the Israeli daily *Hadashot*, writer Sarah Laybobis-Dar interviewed a number of Israelis who knew of the use of bacteriological weapons in 1948. One of those interviewed, Uri Mileshtin, an official historian for the Israeli Defense Forces, said that bacteria was used to poison the wells of every village emptied of its Arab inhabitants. According to Mileshtin, it was former Israeli Defense Minister Moshe Dayan who gave the order in 1948 to remove Arabs from their villages, bulldoze their homes, and render their water wells unusable with typhus and dysentery bacteria.

We also know of this anti-civilian warfare from a former Zionist, Naeim Giladi. Writing in the April-May 1998 issue of *The Link*, Giladi tells of a conversation he had in the early 1950s with a technician with Mekorot, the Israeli Water Authority. The technician was testing a well near a construction site where Giladi was working. Giladi asked him what he was doing. Thinking Giladi had fought in 1948, the technician replied: "Don't you remember? We used bacteria in many places. Every village we occupied we put bacteria in the wells. Now we keep testing them to keep track of when it is safe to use them again."

The subject of Israel's use of poison gained worldwide headlines in November 1999, when Suha Arafat, wife of Yassir Arafat, made the accusation at the opening of a U.S.-sponsored health project for Palestinian women in Ramallah, at which First Lady Hillary Clinton was present. At one point Mrs. Arafat said: "Our people have been submitted to the daily and intensive use of poisonous gas by the Israeli forces which has led to an increase in cancer cases among women and children."

The U.S. media denounced Mrs. Clinton for not immediately registering her dissent to what some columnists called a blood libel against the Jewish people. Few, if any, examined the allegations.

Israel's deadly use of tear gas to put down the Palestinian intifada of 1987-1993 first raised the question of whether Israel was using chemical weapons that cause injuries and fetal deaths. The Database Project on Palestinian Human Rights reported that, as of 31 May, 1988:

> More than 50 people have died after tear gas inhalation; 2 people have lost organs after being directly hit by canisters; and at least 150 pregnant women have suffered miscarriages or intrauterine fetal death after being gassed. A four-year-old boy was burned to death in Gaza City when a gas canister fired into his home ignited a kerosene stove; two of his siblings were badly burned and hospitalized.

Both *The Washington Post* and *The New York Times* of 16 January 1988 reported that Israeli soldiers, contrary to instructions printed clearly on the canisters not to use the tear gas inside buildings, did use them in hospitals and places of worship. The most dangerous use was in closed areas, such as shops and homes, an act that could and did produce fatalities. *The Washington Post* of 31 May 1988 reported:

> Palestinian doctors and officials working for the UN Relief and Works Agency (UNRWA)… contend there have been more than 1,200 injuries, dozens of miscarriages and at least 11 deaths from tear gas since the uprising began December 9 [1987].

And *The Washington Post* of 14 April 1988 concluded that there appears to be:

> … much evidence indicating that on numerous occasions soldiers and police have violated the manufacturer's printed warning by firing the gas into enclosed areas such as rooms or small courtyards.

These reports of Israeli misuse of tear gas prompted the Pennsylvania supplier, TransTechnology, to suspend sales of tear gas to Israel on 6 May 1988. The tear gas canisters, however, were still in use as of November 1989, but without the manufacturer's name on them. And one year after the suspension, *The Jerusalem Post* of 27 April 1989 reported that the investigative arm of the U.S. Congress had found that no grounds existed for withholding U.S. export of tear gas to Israel, "despite reports that the IDF [Israeli Defense Forces] had sometimes used it improperly in the West Bank."

In 1990, The Swedish Save the Children organization sponsored a major report, "The Status of Palestinian Children during the Uprising in the Occupied Territories." The report concluded that Israeli use of tear gas had "contaminated homes, schools, offices, mosques, churches, clinics, and hospitals," and that decontamination was "extremely difficult" for a number of reasons:[8]

    a. First, most Palestinians were not told by the Israeli military government's Civil Administration how to decontaminate their houses, schools, or their buildings; in fact, no school official interviewed said that decontamination had been carried out in the many schools hit with tear gas.

    b. Second, many, if not most Palestinians could not obtain, let alone afford, the dry cleaning services suggested by the Pennsylvania manufacturer.

    c. Third, according to field investigations by the DataBase Project on Palestinian Human Rights, some Palestinian water sources, such as wells, were contaminated by the introduction of tear gas canisters.

    d. Fourth, because most rural and refugee families traditionally stored a year's worth of foodstuffs, ingested foods contaminated by tear gas had the long-term potential of causing vomiting and diarrhea.

A report by Physicians for Human Rights further suggested that exposure to CS gas (the "irritant agent" type of tear gas that is the only type known to have been used during the first intifada) can result in heart failure, liver damage, and other long-term chronic illnesses, including carcinogenicity and influence on fertility.[9]

The *Save the Children Report* concluded with these chilling words from yet another report in the *Journal of the American Medical Association:*

    From a toxicological perspective, there is a great need for epidemiologic and more laboratory research that would illuminate the full health consequence of exposure to tear gas compounds such as CS. The possibility of long-term health consequences such as tumor formation, reproductive effects, and pulmonary disease is especially disturbing in view of the multiple exposures sustained by demonstrators and non-demonstrators alike in some areas of civilian unrest.

Now, with the second intifada, gas attacks against Palestinians again proliferate. Michael Finkel, writing in *The New York Times Magazine* of 24 December 2000, describes a typical scenario:

> At one point, following a rock-throwing jag, there was a sudden series of suction-like pops. "Fireworks!" the kids shouted, and in an instant tear-gas canisters exploded about us. For reasons that didn't seem clear, the Israeli retaliation had begun… "Look," said Hares [a young teenager], making a face. "Built in America. I hate America." The writing on the outside of the 560 CS Long-Range Projectile said that it was manufactured by Federal Laboratories in Pittsburgh.

And there are other troubling reports. Israel admits sending secret units into the West Bank and Gaza Strip, according to the investigative journalist Gordon Thomas in his article "Banned Toxins Are Israel's New Weapon Against the Palestinians," published in *Al-Sharq al-Awsat* on 31 October 2000. What Israel doesn't admit is that these units are equipped with various types of weapons, all of which are banned under international treaties.

The weapons include fast-acting toxins that leave no obvious traces and can be treated only by specialists who know how to detect them.

At least six types of these toxins have been created and developed at Israel's Biological Research Institute, located 12 miles southeast of Tel Aviv. They were employed in September 1997, when Israel's intelligence agency, Mossad, tried to assassinate Khalid Mish'al, a Hamas leader, in Amman, Jordan. When the operation failed, the Institute's chemical experts created more advanced delivery systems.

One such system is a powerful revolver that fires the toxins from a range of 150 feet. When the bullet hits the target, it injects a needle containing the toxin. Israeli operatives are trained to hit body parts, excluding the head, where the needle leaves no trace. The gun itself is silenced and the round is designed to penetrate just deeply enough for the toxin to have maximum effect.

The lethal needles essential for the operation have been supplied secretly to the Institute by German Jewish chemists who used to work officially for the Stasi intelligence service in the former East Germany.

The "smoking gun" that confirms Israel's chemical and biological operations showed up on 4 October 1992, at 6:35 p.m., when Israel's El Al Flight LY 1862 crashed into a block of 12-story tenements in Bijlmer, just outside Amsterdam. Killed were three crew members, an unidentified "non-revenue passenger," and at least 43 people on the ground.[10]

At first Israeli and Dutch officials said the El Al flight carried only "perfume and gift articles." As late as 22 April 1998, Israeli Transport Minister Shaul Yahalom insisted there was "no dangerous material on that plane. Israel has nothing to hide."

Meanwhile, since the crash, 850 Bijlmer survivors have been suffering from multiple ailments including fatigue, breathing disorders, hair loss, neurological ailments, mental confusion, depression, encephalomyelitis and joint pains — all of which they blame on the crash.

Then, on 4 October 1998, the Dutch daily *NRC Handelsblat* printed a leaked copy of a page from Flight 1862's cargo manifest. It showed that the plane had 10 tons of chemicals on board, including hydrofluoric acid, isopropanal, and dimethylphosphonate (DMMP) – three of the four chemicals used in the production of sarin nerve gas. Combined, the chemicals aboard Flight 1862 could have killed the entire population of a major world city.

The DMMP had been shipped by Solkatronic Chemicals Inc. of Morrisville, PA and was destined for the Israeli Institute for Biological Research (IIBR) in Nes Ziona, outside Tel Aviv. IIBR is Israel's front organization for the development, testing and production of chemical and biological weapons. The poison (and antidote) used in the attempted assassination of the Hamas leader in Jordan was provided by IIBR. So secret is its location it appears on no maps and is off-limits even to members of the Israeli Parliament.

In the months following the crash, a Dutch citizens' group, Onterzoeksgreg Vliegramp Bijlmermeer (OVB), revealed that, in addition to the three toxic chemicals, traces of uranium, zirconium and lanthanum were found in soil samples taken from the crash site. More alarmingly, OVB found traces of depleted uranium (DU) in feces samples taken from survivors. Swallowing or breathing DU dust can cause significant and long-lasting irradiation of internal tissues, resulting in physical and mental debilities similar to those reported by the Bijlmer survivors.

How seriously should Palestinians-and, indeed, the rest of us on earth- take this unmapped Institute? The answer is provided by a former IIBR biologist in a 4 October 1998 interview with *The London Sunday Times:* "There is hardly a single known or unknown form of chemical or biological weapon ... which is not manufactured at the institute."

If anything, Suha Arafat may have understated the case.

Israel's Anti-Civilian Tanks And Helicopter Gunships

Tiananmen Square, June 4, 1989. A young man, unarmed, stands defiantly before a tank. There's no way he's going to win. Yet he stands there. David against Goliath: the indomitable spirit to be free confronting the forces of oppression. The picture was seen around the world on the covers of news magazines and the front pages of newspapers. Americans, in particular, decried the brutal use of such overwhelming force.

But what of the photo of the Palestinian youngster taken in occupied Palestine in October 2000? There he stands, alone, armed only with a stone, poised defiantly before an on-coming Israeli tank. How many U.S. news magazines carried this photo on its covers? How many newspapers highlighted it on their front pages? Where was the outcry against the use of such force against a civilian population? And what of the follow-up stories?

Periodically, the U.S. media keeps us updated on what is happening to the lone Chinese student. But what of the Palestinian child? How many reports told us how old he was (13 at the time) — or even his name — it was Faris Odeh? More incredibly, how many newspapers or TV outlets reported that, nine days after his heroic stand, Faris Odeh was fatally shot in the neck by an Israeli sharpshooter?

Arab-Americans often speculate that, were the situation reversed, how different the coverage would have been. Imagine that a Jewish population has been suffering for 50 years under an Arab military occupation; imagine that Arab settlers were colonizing more and more Jewish land; that at some point the Jews rise up in protest; that the Arab occupiers come into their overpopulated cities and camps with tanks and gunships; that a Jewish child stands valiantly before one of the advancing tanks with nothing but a stone. The stuff of front-page news: a modern-day David defying a monster Goliath.

The sight of tanks and helicopter gunships firing into Palestinian population centers is a terrifying one. Again, few photos of the destroyed homes and buildings have found their way into our media. Some idea of the impact can be had by considering a United Nations estimate that tens of millions of dollars of damage to Palestinian "buildings, infrastructure and vehicles (has resulted) due mainly to the Israeli Army's use of heavy weapons, including rockets, tank shells and high-caliber automatic weapons." The report went on to say that in the first six weeks of the recent conflict, Israeli attacks resulted in the partial or total destruction of 431 private homes, 13 public buildings, 10 factories, and 14 religious buildings.

But there is more to be concerned about. A 1995 report from the U.S. Army Environmental Policy Institute states that Israel is one of the countries with DU munitions in its arsenal. And Israel's U.S.-manufactured Apache and Cobra helicopters are both equipped to fire DU shells. Israel's Sabra tank, modeled on the Abrams M1A1 tank, likewise has the capability of firing DU shells.

DU is a waste product of the process that produces enriched uranium for use in atomic weapons and nuclear power plants. When turned into a metal it can be used to make a shell that penetrates steel. It is also pyrophoric, so that it burns when heated by friction when it strikes steel. And when it does that, it spews tiny particles of poisonous and radioactive uranium oxide into the air. These small particles can then be ingested or inhaled by humans for miles around. Just one particle, when lodged in a vital organ, can be dangerous.

At least one monitoring organization in the United States, the International Action Center (IAC), founded by former U.S. Attorney General Ramsey Clark, has called for an international investigation of the use by Israel of depleted uranium shells in its repression of the latest Palestinian uprising. According to IAC co-director Sara Flounders:

> Such use of DU weapons adds to the crimes the Israeli forces are committing against the Palestinian population. Israeli helicopter gunships are firing into densely populated areas. According to international law these attacks on civilian areas are

war crimes, as is the long-term destruction of the environment from depleted uranium contamination. The radioactive materials enter into the land, the water, and the whole food chain, contaminating the densely-populated West Bank and Gaza, where water is a scarce resource. The wanton radioactive contamination of this region is a crime against all of humanity and a threat to the entire region now and for generations to come.[11]

Perhaps this was what Suha Arafat had in mind.

Civilians in the Crosshairs

The weapons we have examined are all being used against a Palestinian civilian population. Israel claims it uses these weapons as means of crowd control. But Israel uses these weapons *only* against Palestinian crowds. It *never* uses them against Jewish demonstrators or rioters inside Israel or against Jewish settlers in the West Bank or Gaza. Palestinians claim this is blatant anti-Arab racism.

A 13 December, 2000 article by Lee Hockstader in *The Washington Post* quoted the defense correspondent of the Israeli newspaper Haaretz as reporting that "Key members of the [Israeli] defense establishment are increasingly convinced that Israel has frequently been using excessive force against the Palestinians." Hockstader cites another article in the Israeli paper *Maariv* that describes two army combat units in which soldiers repeatedly opened fire indiscriminately, exaggerating the threat they faced to secure the approval of commanders who were not at the scene.

And among the civilians in the crosshairs, certain categories of individuals are targeted:

Children. As of 1 December 2000, 310 people have been killed in clashes between Israelis and Palestinians including 97 children aged 18 or under who were all Palestinians, according to the UN Children's Fund, UNICEF. UNICEF spokeswoman Lynn Geldof also reported that 9,802 Palestinians had been injured in the violence from the end of September until November 30, of which an estimated 4,116 were children.[12]

Stories and photos of killed and wounded children have filled the Arab media, but one of the most poignant reports I have read came from a 28 October 2000 article by *Chicago Tribune* staff writer Stephen Franklin.

He quotes medical social worker Magada Abu Ghosh, who had been pressed into service as a first-aid worker. She had been standing beside one of the ambulances, waiting to take the wounded off on stretchers. "I heard a loud noise," she recalled, "and I looked around and there was this boy, maybe he was 17 years old. I will never forget him. He was wearing a white T-shirt. The bullets exploded in his leg and his hand and the blood was all over him. He was just standing there and he didn't realize what happened. He died."

And Michael Finkel, in his previously cited *New York Times Magazine* article, reported that he spent two weeks at Karni crossing in Gaza with stone-throwers 13, 14 and 15 years of age, and each day the Israeli army fired live ammunition at the kids, even though "Not once did I see or hear a single shot from the Palestinian side." What about Israel's claim that its Army fires only in self-defense? Finkel writes: "Never during the time I spent at Karni did an Israeli soldier appear to be in mortal danger. Nor was either an Israeli soldier or settler even slightly injured. In that two-week period, at least 11 Palestinians were killed during the day at Karni."

Medical Personnel. Magada Abu Ghosh's position was itself dangerous. On 28 November 2000, Physicians for Human Rights-Israel issued a report "Medicine Under Fire, October 2000." In it, the world-wide human rights organization accused Israeli security forces of using rubber and rubber-coated steel bullets, as well as live firearms, against Palestinian civilians, including doctors and ambulance drivers who were trying to evacuate other Palestinian civilians who had been injured. Much of the world did see the shooting death of 12-year-old Muhammed al-Durreh, as he huddled next to his father. What the world did not see was the shooting death of the ambulance medic who had tried to reach him.[13]

"It is becoming very difficult to evacuate the injured," said Dr. Mohammad Skaft, head of the first-aid teams in the West Bank. Ambulances are hit by gunfire, emergency workers are wounded, and field hospitals, many of them close to the clashes, fall under the clouds of tear gas fired at the crowds. "When you get hit with the gas, said one emergency worker, "you can't do anything. You can't breathe."

The Physicians for Human Rights-Israel report also criticized Israeli security forces for delaying ambulances and medical relief vehicles on their way to evacuation of the injured and for harassing the medical relief personnel.

Journalists. Many of the journalists, particularly photographers and cameramen from the local and international media, have been chased, intimidated and shot by Israeli security forces in order to prevent them from documenting the killing and wounding of defenseless civilians. According to the Palestinian Center for Human Rights, these incidents multiplied after a French journalist filmed the killing of Muhammed al-Durreh. Such practices are expressly condemned by international conventions and law. The Palestinian Center for Human Rights (PCHR) has documented numerous such violations on its web site www.pchrgaza.org. We note just a few:[14]

- On 11 November, 2000, Yola Monakhov, 26, an American photographer for the Associated Press, was crouched in a doorway near Rachel's Tomb in Bethlehem. Suddenly an Israeli soldier appeared from around a corner about 50 yards away, aimed at her and fired. There had been no gunfire from the Palestinian side, she said from her hospital bed, following two operations to treat extensive damage to her pelvis.

- Israeli soldiers beat Awadh Awadh, a photographer for *Agence France Presse,* and tried to break his camera while he was covering clashes with Palestinian civilians on 29 September 2000. On the same day, Israeli soldiers shot Amer El-Jabari, a reporter for NBC, wounding him with a bullet in the head as he covered clashes in Hebron.

- On 4 October 2000, Atta Oweisat, a photographer for the Zoom 77 press agency, was attacked by seven Israeli soldiers while he was covering a funeral procession of a Palestinian martyr in the village of Jabal El-Mukabber. The soldiers forced Oweisat to the ground and began hitting him in the stomach and neck. Oweisat fainted and had to be taken to the hospital.

- On 9 October 2000, in Ramallah, Israeli troops shot rubber-coated steel bullets at Luce Delahye, a *Newsweek* photographer, hitting the lens of his camera. A week later, also in Ramallah, Delahye was hit by a rubber-coated bullet in the forehead, while he was photographing a youngster who had been hit in the head.

- On 31 October 2000, Ben Wedeman, an American correspondent for CNN, was covering a Palestinian demonstration near Al Mentar (Karmi) Outlet. The situation had been relatively calm until the Israeli forces started shooting intensively and "walking" tank shells in the direction of Wedeman and other journalists.

Wedeman, who was wearing a helmet and bulletproof vest, was forced to lie down to escape the shooting. A few minutes after the shooting broke out, and while he was trying to stand up with his back to the Israelis, he was wounded with a live bullet in his right side and had to be evacuated to Shifa' hospital.

In light of these incidents — and they are but a few of the ones documented — the PCHR has called upon the international community, especially the High Contracting Parties to the Fourth Geneva Convention, to implement UN Security Council Resolution 1322/2000, which calls for establishing an international commission of inquiry to investigate the actions of the Israeli Defense Forces. Israel rejects such a UN-designated commission, opting instead for a three-person commission headed by former U.S. Senator George Mitchell, which Israel insists will be permitted only to consult the findings of other researchers, and not gather information itself.

Certainly, Senator Mitchell's panel would be expected to consult the findings of the respected human rights organizations listed below. And the hope is that, once it has read these reports, Senator Mitchell will insist that Israel allow his commission to conduct its own inquiry into the allegations.

International Law on the Treatment of Civilians

The renowned international lawyer W. Thomas Mallison liked to quote the Roman philosopher/ emperor Marcus Aurelius, who observed that the only thing separating men from the jungle is the law. That truth was brought home to Americans in the wake of our post-presidential election this past November, 2000. How often were we reminded that we are a nation of laws, and that it is only our respect for the law that keeps us from social meltdown.

Nations, too, have acknowledged this principle in their relations with one another. Between 1864-1949, a series of treaties were signed in Geneva, Switzerland, providing for humane treatment of combatants and civilians in wartime.

The first convention, signed by 16 nations, covered the protection of sick and wounded soldiers and medical personnel and facilities. Later conventions extended the first to naval warfare (1906) and to the treatment of prisoners of war (1929). As a result of World War II, four conventions were adopted in 1949 (including by Israel) to strengthen and codify earlier treaties and safeguard civilians.

It is these treaties that Israel has been charged with violating by various international organizations:

Amnesty International, United Kingdom:

> Since 29 September (until 5 November 2000) 130 Palestinians have been killed by the Israeli security forces, nearly 40 of them children, during riots and demonstrations in Israel and the Occupied Territories. Amnesty International has sent two missions to Israel and the Occupied Territories to investigate the excessive use of force by the Israeli security forces. The first mission produced a report concluding that Israeli security forces had repeatedly used lethal force in situations where there was no apparent danger to themselves or others. Amnesty International is calling on the United Nations to establish urgently an independent international investigation, to include criminal justice experts known for their impartiality and integrity, and to investigate all killings of civilians that have taken place since 29 September in Israel, the Occupied Territories and south Lebanon.
>
> Amnesty International UK today calls on the British government to suspend all exports or transfers of components, spares, servicing and equipment for U.S.-supplied attack helicopters in Israel until the Israeli authorities demonstrate that the helicopters will not be used to commit human rights violations in Israel and the Occupied Territories and the areas under the control of the Palestinian Authority. Israeli forces have used U.S.-supplied helicopter gunships to violate the human rights of Palestinians in punitive attacks — on civilians, including children — where there was no imminent danger to life. - *Report dated 24 October 2000.*

Amnesty International, USA:

> Amnesty International USA today called on the U.S. government to cease all transfers of attack helicopters to Israel, including the pending sale of Apache helicopters, until Israeli authorities demonstrate that the helicopters will not be used to commit human rights violations in Israel and the Occupied

Territories and the areas under the control of the Palestine Authority. - *Report dated 19 October 2000.*

In policing the recent demonstrations, the Israeli security forces tended to use military methods rather than policing methods involving the protection of human lives. - *Report dated 19 October 2000.*

Amnesty International reiterated its urgent call for an independent international investigation by the United Nations into the serious human rights abuses in Israel and the Occupied Territories, including the areas under the jurisdiction of the Palestinian Authority, since 29 September. - *Report dated 13 October 2000.*

Amnesty International today expressed grave concern for the safety of civilians, following Israeli military helicopter attacks in Gaza City and Ramallah which reported injured Palestinian civilians. - *Report dated 12 October 2000.*

Since 29 September, Israeli security forces have frequently used excessive force on demonstrators when lives were not in immediate danger. - *Report dated 9 October 2000.*

Amnesty International condemns indiscriminate killings of civilians following four days of clashes in Israel and the Occupied Territories which have left at least 35 Palestinian civilians dead and hundreds of others injured. The dead civilians, among them young children, include those uninvolved in the conflict and seeking safety. The loss of civilian life is devastating and this is compounded by the fact that many appear to have been killed or injured as a result of the use of excessive or indiscriminate force. - *Report dated 2 October 2000.*

B'Tselem: The Israeli Information Center for Human Rights:

…Testimonies given to B'Tselem indicate that security forces often fire "rubber bullets" at times with fatal results in violation of the Open-Fire Regulations (that such bullets should be used only as a last resort to disperse riots and demonstrations, that they should be aimed only at the legs, that they should not be fired at a distance of less than 40 meters, and not at children.) In some cases, the security forces themselves admit the breach of regulations.

New York Times correspondent Joel Greenberg was an eye-witness to the shooting death of eight-year old Ali Jawarish and provided testimony to B'Tselem:

> When the soldier fired, he was some 15 to 20 meters from the fleeing children. At that time, some children were detained and others were fleeing, no stones were thrown. After the firing, the soldiers retreated. When they did so, I noticed a child, around nine or ten years old, lying motionless on the ground.

In the vast majority of cases in which soldiers shot "rubber bullets" and killed Palestinians, no one was held accountable. Forty-nine of the 57 cases of Palestinians killed by "rubber bullets" involved IDF soldiers. In only three of these cases did the authorities initiate legal action against those responsible ... [Of those soldiers found guilty of killing Palestinians], one was acquitted, one sentenced to 21-months' imprisonment and two years' probation; and one subject to disciplinary proceedings. - *Report dated 24 November 1998.*

Human Rights Watch, World Report 2000:

Human Rights Watch reports its week-long investigation of clashes in the West Bank, Gaza, and northern Israel showed repeated use by Israeli security forces of lethal force in situations where demonstrators posed no threat of death or serious injury to security forces or others. In situations where Palestinians did fire upon Israeli security forces, the IDF showed a troubling proclivity to resort to indiscriminate lethal force in response. At least 100 Palestinians have been killed and 3,500 injured in clashes with Israeli security forces. Human Rights Watch also expresses concern at the IDF's use of medium caliber munitions, which are meant for penetrating concrete and other hard surface barriers, against unarmed demonstrators in the West Bank and Gaza Strip. The military munitions were particularly devastating when they hit civilians.

The organization also condemned the repeated apparent targeting of emergency medical personnel and facilities by the IDF, as well as stoning attacks by Palestinian and Israeli civilians on ambulances.

Under international standards on the use of force by law enforcement officials, firearms may be used only "in self-defense or defense of others against the imminent threat of death or serious injury." Even then, law enforcement officials must "exercise restraint in such use and act in proportion to the seriousness of the offence and the legitimate objective to be achieved," and "minimize damage and injury, and respect and preserve human life."

Civilians should not be dying in this conflict, on either side," said Hanny Megally, executive director of the Middle East and North Africa division of Human Rights Watch ... Megally noted that under the Fourth Geneva Convention, which governs military occupations, Palestinians in the West Bank, the Gaza Strip, and East Jerusalem are internationally protected persons, and signatory states have an obligation to respect and ensure respect for rights and guarantees of the Convention.

MADRE, International Women's Human Rights Organization:

As of 9 October 2000, at least 85 Palestinians have been killed and over 3,000 wounded by Israeli forces using rubber-coated bullets, live ammunition, helicopter gunships, tanks and anti-tank missiles.

In an interview given to *The New York Times* on 4 October 2000, Dr. Khaled Qurie, director of Makassed Hospital in East Jerusalem, reports an unusually high number of upper body injuries to the head, neck, chest and abdomen compared with previous clashes. Doctors at St. John's hospital in Jerusalem have treated 18 Palestinians shot in the eye at close range with rubber-coated bullets. This, despite the fact that Israeli troops are trained to fire these bullets from at least 100 feet away and only at the feet and legs. International standards dictate that security forces may use firearms only when lives are threatened and other options are unavailable. In these confrontations, Israeli forces have apparently relied on deadly force as a first, rather than last, resort. Palestinian human rights organizations report that numerous people who were seeking shelter from the clashes have been among those fatally wounded by indiscriminate Israeli gunfire.

The Union of Palestinian Medical Relief Committees reports that a full 44% of the wounded are children under the age of 18.

It is our view that the conduct of the Israeli military violates numerous international human rights standards, including Articles 9, 10 and 11 of the United Nations Basic Principles on the Use of Force and Firearms by Law Enforcement Officials and Articles of the Fourth Geneva Convention governing the treatment of civilians under military occupation.

Mary Robinson, UN Human Rights Commissioner:

The civilian population feels besieged by a stronger power prepared to use its superior force against demonstrations and stone-throwing by adolescents … It's very clear it's having a devastating effect on the civilian population. - *News Conference, Geneva, 27 November 2000.*

Conclusion

One question that haunts this report throughout is why do civilians, particularly children, expose themselves to such high-tech death and destruction?

Israelis blame Palestinian parents for sending their children out to die. But that wasn't the case with the mother of Faris Odeh, the 13-year-old who confronted the tank. She didn't want her son standing in front of sharpshooters. When Faris was killed, she wept uncontrollably.

Yet Mrs. Odeh and the other parents of slain Palestinian children know why their children throw stones. I'm reminded of a quote from Alexander Solzhenitsyn's "You only have power over people so long as you don't take everything away from them. But when you've robbed a man of everything, he's no longer in your power — he's free again."

Palestinian hopes of shaking off the 50-plus years of military occupation have collapsed over the years, especially since the 1993 Oslo Accords; Israel to this day continues to confiscate more and more Palestinian land for the construction of Jewish-only settlements and Jewish-only highways, leaving Palestinians penned up in their ever denser bantustans. Intifadas erupt when the oppressed know they have nothing to lose. It happens often enough in the history of anti-colonial conflicts, in South Africa, Vietnam, Ireland, Algeria, to name but a few.

It is an imperative that knows no one religion, nor one cultural ethos. It is a cry from the human heart. When American revolutionaries rebelled from their oppressors, they described it as their rightful claim to life, *liberty* and the pursuit of happiness. Palestinians are no different.

Occupiers too have instinctive feelings. They know that land acquired by illegitimate force can only be held by the threat of superior arms. That's why the United States gives Israel some $10 billion a year, as documented by Richard Curtiss in our September 1997 *Link*, in order to maintain its military andeconomic superiority. And that's why Israel has reacted to this latest Palestinian intifada by using what the international community has deemed excessive military force against a civilian population.

Seldom, however, do occupiers comprehend Count von Bismarck's admonition that you can do everything with a bayonet except sit on it.

So the madness continues.

End Notes

[1] Ezrahi, Yaron, "Rubber Bullets: Power and Consensus in Modern Israel," 1997, *Univ. of California Press*, p. 214.

[2] O'Sullivan, Arieh, in *The Jerusalem Post*, 27 October 2000.

[3] Palestine Red Crescent Society Web Site <www.palestiners.org/bullet_types_images.htm>. On same Site, see PRCS Director Mohamed Awad's medical analysis of the extensive damage caused by rubber-coated steel bullets and other blast weapons.

[4] Copy of the *B'Tselem Report* can be found on the web at <www.btselem.org/files/ERubber.rtf>.

[5] See *B'Tselem Report* noted above.

[6] See *B'Tselem Report* noted above.

[7] Kiley, Sam, in *The London Times*, 17 October 2000.

[8] Nixon, Anne, "The Status of Palestinian Children during the Uprising in the Occupied Territories, Part I: Child Death and Injury," Rädda Barnen, *Swedish Save the Children*, January 1990. This is one of the most comprehensive studies on the physical and long-term effects of the type of tear gas used by Israel.

[9] See *Save the Children* Report above.

[10] Smith, Gar, "Uranium Skies: What was aboard Flight 1862?" in *Earth Island Journal*, v. 14, no. 4, winter '99-2000. Information on the crash is based on this article.

[11] Flounders, Sare & Catalinotto, John, "Is the Israeli Military Using Depleted Uranium Weapons Against the Palestinians?" International Action Center, November 2000. See Web Site <www.iacenter.org>.

[12] *Agence France Presse*, 1 December 2000.

[13] "Medicine Under Fire-October 2000," *Report by Physicians for Human Rights-Israel.* This Report is based on hundreds of first-hand testimonies by the wounded, eye-witnesses, doctors and other medical personnel. For further information, phone PHR's office in Israel at 011-972-3-5664526.

[14] "Silencing the Press: A Report on Israeli Aggression against Journalists, September 29-November 20, 2000," Palestine Center for Human Rights. See Web Site <www.pchrgaza.org>.

For Israel, Land or Peace

President Jimmy Carter

An underlying reason that years of U.S. diplomacy have failed and violence in the Middle East persists is that some Israeli leaders continue to "create facts" by building settlements in occupied territory. Their deliberate placement as islands or fortresses within Palestinian areas makes the settlers vulnerable to attack without massive military protection, frustrates Israelis who seek peace and at the same time prevents any Palestinian government from enjoying effective territorial integrity.

At Camp David in September 1978, President Anwar Sadat, Prime Minister Menachem Begin and I spent most of our time debating this issue before we finally agreed on terms for peace between Egypt and Israel and for the resolution of issues concerning the Palestinian people. The bilateral provisions led to a comprehensive and lasting treaty between Egypt and Israel, made possible at the last minute by Israel's agreement to remove its settlers from the Sinai. But similar constraints concerning the status of the West Bank and Gaza have not been honored, and have led to continuing confrontation and violence.

The foundation for all my proposals to the two leaders was the official position of the government of the United States, based on international law that was mutually accepted by the United States, Egypt, Israel and other nations, and encapsulated in United Nations Security Council Resolution 242. Our government's legal commitment to support this well-balanced resolution has not changed.

Although the acceptance of Resolution 242 was a contentious issue at Camp David, Prime Minister Begin ultimately acknowledged its applicability, "in all its parts." The text emphasizes "the inadmissibility of the acquisition of territory by war and the need to work for a just and lasting peace in which every State in the area can live in security." It requires the "withdrawal of Israeli armed forces from territories occupied in the recent [1967] conflict" and the right of every state in the area "to live in peace within secure and recognized boundaries free from threats or acts of force."

It was clear that Israeli settlements in the occupied territories were a direct violation of this agreement and were, according to the long-stated American position, both "illegal and an obstacle to peace."

Accordingly, Prime Minister Begin pledged that there would be no establishment of new settlements until after the final peace negotiations were completed. But later, under Likud pressure, he declined to honor this commitment, explaining that his presumption had been that all peace talks would be concluded within three months.

There were some notable provisions in the Camp David Accords that related to Palestinian autonomy and the occupation of land. A key element was that "the Israeli military government and its civilian administration will be withdrawn as soon as a self-governing authority has been freely elected by the inhabitants of these areas to replace the existing military government." This transition period was triggered by an election in the occupied territories in January 1996, approved by the Palestinians and the government of Israel and monitored by the Carter Center. Eighty-eight Palestinian Council members were elected, with Yasser Arafat as president, and this self-governing authority, with limited autonomy, convened for the first time in March 1996.

It was also agreed that once the powers and responsibilities of the self-governing authority were established, "A withdrawal of Israeli armed forces will take place and there will be a redeployment of the remaining Israeli forces into specified security locations."

We decided early during the Camp David talks that it would be impossible to resolve the question of sovereignty over East Jerusalem, but proposed the following paragraph concerning the city, on which we reached full agreement:

> Jerusalem, the city of peace, is holy to Judaism, Christianity, and Islam, and all peoples must have free access to it and enjoy the free exercise of worship and the right to visit and transit to the holy places without distinction or discrimination. The holy places of each faith will be under the administration and control of their representatives. A municipal council representative of the inhabitants of the city shall supervise essential functions in the city such as public utilities, public transportation, and tourism and shall ensure that each community can maintain its own cultural and educational institutions.

At the last minute, however, after several days of unanimous acceptance, both Sadat and Begin agreed that there were already enough controversial elements in the accords and requested that this paragraph, although still supported by both sides, be deleted from the final text.

Instead, the two leaders exchanged letters, expressing the legal positions of their respective governments regarding the status of East Jerusalem. They disagreed about sovereignty, of course, but affirmed that the city should be undivided.

As agreed, I informed them that "the position of the United States on Jerusalem remains as stated by Ambassador Arthur Goldberg in the United Nations General Assembly on July 14, 1967, and subsequently by Ambassador Charles Yost in the United Nations Security Council on July 1, 1969." In effect, these statements considered East Jerusalem to be part of the occupied territories, along with the West Bank and Gaza.

The Camp David Accord was signed by all three of us leaders with great fanfare and enthusiasm. President Sadat and Prime Minister Begin embraced warmly at the White House ceremony, and the final document was overwhelmingly ratified by their respective parliaments.

With the inauguration of President Ronald Reagan, there was a period of relative inactivity in the Middle East, except for the Israeli invasion of Lebanon and the subsequent expulsion of PLO forces from Beirut. President Reagan used the announcement of this event on Sept. 1, 1982, to address the nation on the subject of the West Bank and the Palestinians. He stated clearly that "the Camp David agreement remains the foundation of our policy," and his speech included the following declarations:

"The Palestinian inhabitants of the West Bank and Gaza will have full autonomy over their own affairs."

"The United States will not support the use of any additional land for the purpose of settlements during the transition period. Indeed, the immediate adoption of a settlement freeze by Israel, more than any other action, could create the confidence needed for wider participation in these talks. Further settlement activity is in no way necessary for the security of Israel and only diminishes the confidence of the Arabs that a final outcome can be freely and fairly negotiated."

In 1991 there was a major confrontation between the governments of Prime Minister Yitzhak Shamir and President George Bush concerning Israeli settlements in the West Bank, with U.S. threats of withholding financial aid if settlement activity continued. A conference was convened that year in Madrid with participants of the United States, Syria, other Arab nations and some Palestinians who did not officially represent the PLO. At a press conference on Nov. 1, Secretary of State James Baker said, "When we negotiated with Israel, we negotiated on the basis of land for peace, on the basis of total withdrawal from territory in exchange for peaceful relations. . . . This is exactly our position, and we wish it to be applied also in the negotiations between Israelis and Syrians, Israelis and Palestinians. We have not changed our position at all."

Norwegian mediators forged an agreement in September 1993 between Israeli Prime Minister Yitzhak Rabin and Arafat committing both sides to a staged peace process. Although U.S. officials were not involved in this effort, our government commemorated the Oslo Accords in a ceremony at the White House, and built subsequent peace talks on its terms and those of the Camp David Accords. So far, these efforts have not succeeded, and this year there has been a resurgence of violence and animosity between Israelis and Arabs unequaled in more than a quarter of a century. The major issues still to be resolved remain unchanged: the final boundaries of the state of Israel, the return of, or compensation for, Palestinians dislodged from their previous homes and the status of Jerusalem. It seems almost inevitable that the United States will initiate new peace efforts, but it is unlikely that real progress can be made on any of these issues as long as Israel insists on its settlement policy, illegal under international laws that are supported by the United States and all other nations.

There are many questions as we continue to seek an end to violence in the Middle East, but there is no way to escape the vital one: Land or peace?

Jimmy Carter

As an adjunct to Former President Jimmy Carter's insightful article, the following pages provide information about the issue of territorial control within the West Bank. The map on p. 90 also shows the number and location of illegal Jewish settlements in this occupied region. The statistics at the top of p. 91 are insightful, and alarming. The statements by three of the writers quoted pp. 91-93 are taken from materials published by Jews for Justice; information about these publications is given on p. 121.

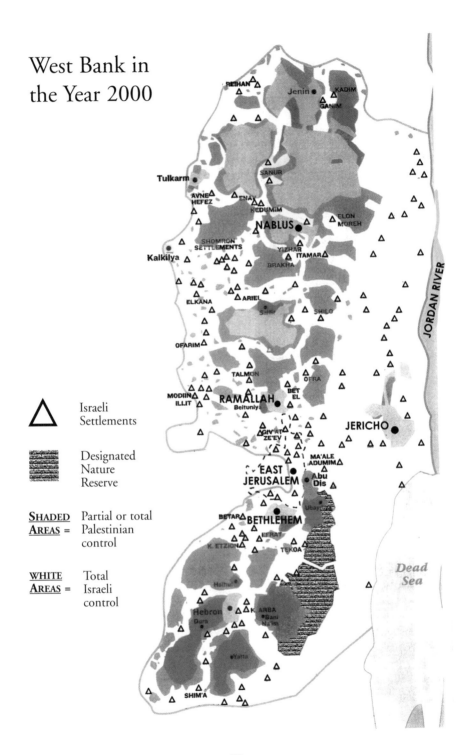

The map on p. 90 shows the West Bank in the year 2000. A little over 17 percent of it is under Palestinian civil and security control; 23.8% is under Palestinian civil control and shared security control with Israel' 59% is under Israeli civil and security control. The Israelis have built approximately 150 settlements in the region, all of which are illegal according to the United Nations.

In the December 1996 issue of *The Link*, Jane Bailey wrote:

"A study of students of Bethlehem University reported by the Coordinating Committee of International NGOs in Jerusalem showed that many families frequently go five days a week without running water... The study goes further to report that, 'water quotas restrict usage by Palestinians living in the West Bank and Gaza, while Israeli settlements have almost unlimited amounts.'

"A summer trip to a Jewish settlement on the edge of the Judean desert less than five miles from Bethlehem confirmed this water inequity for us. While Bethlehemites were buying water from tank trucks at highly inflated rates, the lawns were green in the settlement. Sprinklers were going at mid-day in the hot August sunshine. Sounds of children swimming in the outdoor pool added to the unreality."

The following three statements are taken from *The Israeli Occupation: Background and Analyses of the Current Conflict*, produced by "Jews for Justice in the Middle East." All are by Jewish writers.

Israeli professor describes what is really happening to the Palestinians

"The occupied territories will be divided into 64 isolated territorial cells, each of which will be assigned a special military force, 'and the local commander will have freedom to use his discretion' as to when and who to shoot...but so far there has been only isolation, and not yet 'treatment' inside the cells.

"Now, after the forced restraint of the elections period is over, the Israeli Defense Force and the political system are ready for the 'treatment' phase. And we're talking about a comprehensive 'treatment', which includes not only starvation, imprisonment and 'local discretion' in shooting, but also preplanned personal elimination of the Palestinian leadership and the destruction of the social infrastructure...

"For five months, there has been a process of slow, but systematic and preplanned, elimination of Palestinians in the occupied territories. We won't find it in the statistics of the dead. Israel couldn't get away with thousands of dead. So, soldiers who were carefully trained for the job of conducting a manhunt — aiming at the eyes or knees, in order to injure but not kill, in a daily quota which doesn't distinguish between demonstrators and passersby.

"At least 12,000 injured were reported so far, many of them blind, crippled and maimed. Their fate is to die slowly, far away from the cameras. Some because there are no hospitals to care for them, others because they won't be able to survive, crippled, in the starvation and infrastructure destruction which is inflicted on their people." [*Tanya Reinhart, professor at Tel Aviv University, "We didn't see; We didn't know", March 2001, on Media Monitors Network, http://63.169.91/tanya5html*]

What "closure" means

"Just an hour's drive from Jerusalem, a cruel drama has been underway for the past five months, the likes of which have not been seen since the early period of the Israel occupation, but the Israelis are taking absolutely no interest in it. The iron grip of the closure in its new format is increasingly strangling a population of 2.8 million people, yet no one is saying a word... In the worst of times of the previous Intifada, when the Israeli Defense Force was in every corner and curfew reigned supreme, there was not a situation in which a whole people was jailed without a trial and without the right of appeal...

"Israel has split the West Bank by means of hundreds of trenches, dirt ramparts and concrete cubes which have been placed at the entrance to most of the towns and villages. No one enters and no one leaves, not those who are pregnant and not those who are dying. There isn't even a soldier with whom one can plead and beg. The village, the refugee camp or the town are besieged and their residents are imprisoned...

"A network of bizarre Burma roads that break through the encirclement are sending an entire people along muddy, rocky routes, with the situation aggravated by a substantial risk of getting caught or getting shot by soldiers who often open fire on the desperate travelers trying, somehow, to cling to the routine of their lives. Only those who travel on the roads of the West Bank can grasp the full extent of the atrocity...

"This mass jailing of an entire people, with its monstrously inhumane dimension, entails also a mortal economic blow... The Palestinians are losing $6.8 million a day because of the present closure, and to date their losses total more than a billion dollars. For an economy that was shaky to begin with, that is a death blow...

"Never before has there been distress and suffering on this scale among the Palestinians in the territories. They will engender unprecedented despair and ultimately they will spark violence more cruel and painful than anything seen so far... Their hardship will be transformed into more and more terrorist attacks. This is the point: the horrific distress of the Palestinians because of the present closure will quickly turn into the distress of the Israelis... The current siege, a shamefully appalling operation, must be lifted quickly. This must not be made conditional on the cessation of the violence, because the siege itself is the most effective spur of violence." [*Israeli writer, Gideon Levy, in* Ha'aretz, *March 4, 2001*]

Statement by the Deputy Speaker of the Israeli Knesset, March 2001

"The purposes of the closure policy are as ambiguous as they are counterproductive. Ostensibly, the blockade of Palestinians is meant to curb terrorist acts... But for every terrorist caught in such a net, tens are bred in the morass of hunger, anger and frustration evoked by these pernicious restrictions...

"The damage wrought by the closure is unspeakable. Israel has exposed itself to justifiable international condemnation... And above all, Israel has directly caused untold misery. As long as the territories captured in 1967 are under Israeli control, Israel bears full responsibility for what occurs in those areas. Protestations notwithstanding, the paralysis of Palestinians is an Israeli action, and the moral onus is Israel's to bear – a most shameful and ethically indefensible burden indeed. It should be neither excused nor condoned. The blockades must be lifted and the policy of closures must be stopped now." [*Naomi Chazam, deputy speaker of the Israeli Knesset, in the* Jerusalem Post, *3/16/2001*]

In light of the above statements, though the actions of Palestinian suicide bombers are reprehensible, they are understandable.

The Goals of Zionism in the Light of Christian Scriptures

Harry Wendt

Many Christians, whose approach to the interpretation of the Bible might be described as "fundamentalist," "literalist," or "sectarian," believe:

1. The Jews as an ethnic group are still God's chosen people.
2. Their present claim to the land of Israel is biblically based.
3. Jerusalem will play a special role in the events of the end of time.
4. The Jerusalem Temple will be, and must be, rebuilt.
5. Israel's use of force to achieve its territorial ambitions is biblically justifiable.
6. The weal or woe of any non-Jewish people or nation is determined by its attitude to Israel. If it supports Israel, it will be blessed; if it does not, the opposite will be the case.

The majority of Christians around the world reject these claims.

A. *The Search for Proof-texts*

The title for this essay reflects the fact that there is a difference between what Judaism has in mind when it refers to the Bible, and what Christians have in mind.

Judaism's Bible consists of the Law, the Prophets and the Writings. The Law (or *Torah*) consists of Genesis through Deuteronomy. The Prophets (or *Neviim*) consist of Joshua, Judges, 1 and 2 Samuel, 1 and 2 Kings (*Former Prophets*) and Isaiah, Jeremiah, Ezekiel, and Hosea through Malachi (*Latter Prophets*). The Writings (*Ketubim*) consist of 1 and 2 Chronicles, Ezra, Nehemiah, Esther, Job, Psalms, Proverbs, Ecclesiastes, Song of Solomon, Lamentations, Daniel. (Judaism lists these in the following order: Psalms, Proverbs, Job, Song of Solomon, Ruth, Lamentations, Ecclesiastes, Esther, Daniel, Ezra, Nehemiah, 1 and 2 Chronicles.) Judaism refers to its sacred writings as *TaNaK* – a word made up of the first letter of *Torah, Neviim* and *Ketubim*.

The Christian Scriptures consist of the above, plus the writings Christians refer to as the New Testament and which contains twenty seven books: four Gospels, Acts, Paul's letters, general letters, and Revelation.

A key issue for Christians is: How are we to interpret the Jewish scriptures in the light of the person and ministry of Jesus of Nazareth, whom Christians believe to have been the Messiah – a conviction which Judaism rejects?

Some Christians argue that the difference between the Jewish and Christian scriptures should create no problems in discussions concerning Zionist claims to the "Holy Land," because the majority of Bible passages which (supposedly) speak to the issues under discussion are Old Testament passages anyway. Each passage can have only one meaning, regardless of whether it is interpreted by a Jew or a Christian. Their interpretive principle is: "All Scripture must be taken at face value. What it says, it says – and that's it."

However, Christians who wish to understand the relevance of any Old Testament text for today must filter that Old Testament passage through the mind of Jesus the Messiah. They must know what Jesus and the *New* Testament do with an *Old* Testament opinion, teaching, doctrine, or hope. That process alone can determine what a Christian is to believe and confess. To illustrate this point, we shall survey the hopes expressed in Isaiah 60:1-61:6, and note how Jesus deals with those hopes in his first sermon in Nazareth, his home town, Luke 4:16-30.

Isaiah 60:1-61:6 speaks to Jews who had been taken into exile in Babylon but had but recently returned to Jerusalem. The prophet tells the people that the Lord's glory will soon surround Jerusalem and his people, and nations and kings will come to them, 60:1-3. Jerusalem's scattered children will soon return to her, v.9. The treasures and wealth of the nations will be brought to them by ships across the seas, and camels across the deserts, vv. 5,6,8,9. Even animals brought from other countries will be acceptable for sacrifice in the Temple, v. 7. The very foreigners who destroyed Jerusalem will rebuild Jerusalem, v. 10. Jerusalem's gates will always be open that other nations might bring their wealth to those living within its walls, v. 11. Any nation that will not serve the restored community will be destroyed, v. 12. Timbers from Lebanon will once again be used to beautify the about-to-be-restored Temple, v.13. Those who once despised Jerusalem will honor it, and those living in the newly restored community will suck the milk of the nations, the breasts of kings, vv. 14-16. The restored Jerusalem will surpass Solomon's city in beauty and tranquility, vv. 17,18. God's glory will continually illumine the joyful city, vv.19,20. Those living within its walls will be righteous, possess the Promised Land forever, and greatly increase in numbers.

Indeed, there is only good news for those who had been oppressed and broken in spirit, 61:1. God will pour out his wrath on those who had oppressed them (v. 2), and their pain will be replaced by joy, vv. 3,4. Non-Jews will now do all the necessary menial tasks for God's people so that they in turn might devote themselves to worshiping their God and enjoying the treasures brought to them by surrounding nations, vv. 5,6. Indeed, those who had experienced double shame will now experience double joy, v.7.

When asked to preach in the synagogue in Nazareth, his home-town (Luke 4:16-30), Jesus read *selectively* from the passage referred to above. He omitted all reference to vengeance, to the wealth of the world flowing to Jerusalem and the Temple, and to the Gentiles serving the Jews. He also pointed out that though there had been many needy widows in Israel during the time of Elijah, the prophet went to the aid of a Syro-Phoenician widow (a Gentile!) rather than to one in Israel. And though there were many lepers in Israel during the time of Elisha, the prophet healed Naaman the Syrian (a Gentile!). The response was that those who heard Jesus sought to throw him off a cliff! They objected strongly to the manner in which Jesus re-interpreted passages that encapsulated their cherished hopes.

In short, what the Old Testament says is one thing. Jesus' "final verdict" in relation to those writings is often another thing.

B. *Under the Gentile Heel*

One can well empathize with Jews of today who long to have a land of their own. Their history has indeed been a troubled and painful one. For centuries their attention has focused on that small sweep of land Israel presently occupies. One understands their desire to be permitted to live in that land and to have secure borders in that land, when one knows a little about their history.

Other essays in this volume make sufficient reference to the Jews in the land of Israel in the New Testament era – particularly during this past and present century. Illustration 1 depicts the larger sweep of history. It shows how Old Testament Israel was ruled in turn by the Assyrians, Babylonians, Persians, Greeks and Romans. During this vast sweep of history, the nation rarely enjoyed independence. Though Israel's overlords changed frequently, the nation's lot under those overlords rarely changed. The illustration makes no reference to relations between Egypt and Israel during the period depicted, nor does it make reference

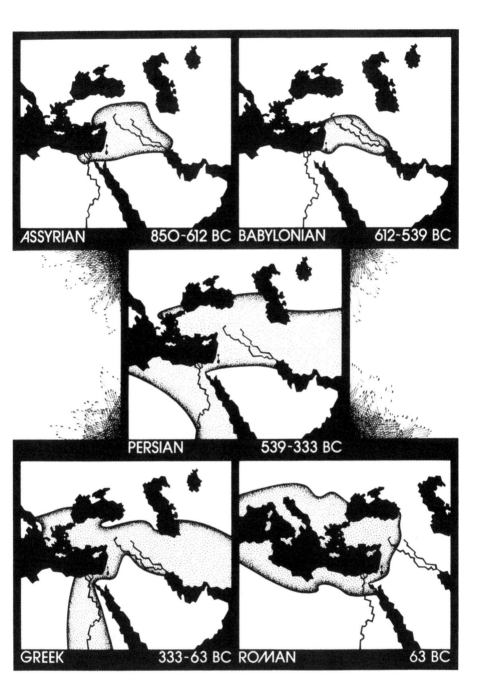

Illustration 1

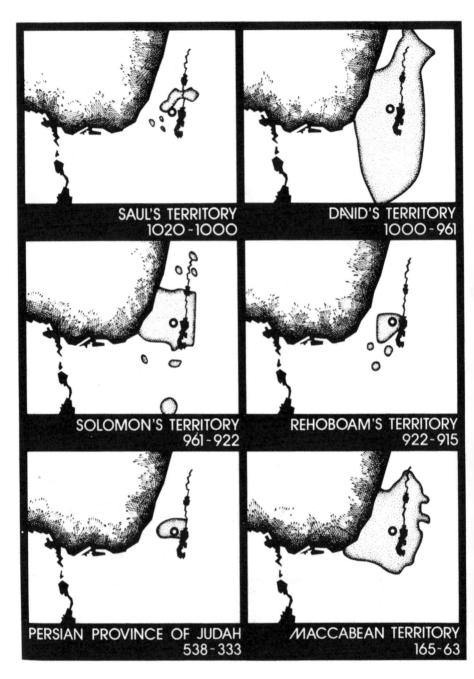

Illustration 2

to the Ptolemies and Seleucids who ruled the area from the time of the death of Alexander the Great in 323 B.C. until about 142 B.C.

C. Borders Increase – Borders Decrease

Many who rely upon what they were taught in Sunday School for their biblical insights are content to believe that after Israel entered the land under Joshua and subdued the local inhabitants, the conquest was complete (Joshua 11:23), and the area controlled by Israel was extensive. However, numerous passages in Joshua suggest that the conquest was anything but complete, Joshua 13:1,13; 15:63; 16:10; 17:12,16-18; 23:4-8; Judges 1:1-2:10. To complicate matters, the Joshua narrative reports only the capture of the territory of Benjamin (chs. 6-8) and Judah, chs. 9,10. Apart from that, we are told only that some who had not taken part in the Exodus from Egypt linked up with the invaders (8:30-35), and that the fortress of Hazor to the north of the Sea of Galilee was captured, ch. 11. One might well ask: Does Joshua report what *actually took place* in the conquest, or does it report how the writer felt the conquest *should have been carried out?*

Many believe that Joshua reports an initial entry into the land, and that Judges then outlines a gradual infiltration. After all, despite the "conquest" outlined in Joshua, according to Judges the Canaanites seem to be everywhere, and intermarriage took place (Judges 3:5,6) – with the result that many Israelites worshiped Canaanite gods. Because the judges came from a variety of tribes, it seems likely that most, if not all, of them ruled limited areas and dealt with local problems and threats. At times, relations between tribes on the east and west banks of the Jordan were anything but good, Joshua 22.

Though frame 1 in illustration 2 suggests that Saul, Israel's first king, ruled only a limited area, other passages suggest that he conquered the territory that his successor David eventually ruled, 1 Samuel 14:47,48. Certainly Saul was not a monarch in the modern sense of the word. He was out plowing his fields with oxen when news reached him about the plight of Jabesh-Gilead, 1 Samuel 11:1-5.

The frames that follow in illustration 2 depict how Israel's boundaries changed during the Old Testament period after Saul. Again, the borders suggested are approximate.

When David came to power, the situation changed. Eventually David established a realm of considerable size. Its borders coincided approximately with those outlined in Genesis 15:18-21.

Though Solomon inherited his father's realm, in the latter years of his reign its borders began to shrink (frame 3) as nations David captured regained their independence, e.g., the Edomites and the Syrians; see 1 Kings 11:14,23, 26ff. It seems that Solomon exploited the Northern Kingdom to support his building ventures; he had twelve officers over the north, but only one over the south, 1 Kings 4:7,19. It is not surprising that the north broke away after his death, 1 Kings 12:1-24. After all, the north had previously revolted from no less a personage than David himself, 2 Samuel 20.

Rehoboam, Solomon's son, ruled territory much smaller than anything David or Solomon had controlled (frame 4). It consisted of only Judah and Benjamin, 2 Kings 12:23. The Northern Kingdom was now ruled by Jeroboam. Even if both north and south are taken into consideration, Israel's territorial holdings had by now diminished greatly.

The postexilic province of Judah was but a pale shadow of what the realm had been in its heyday under David. Naturally, many looked back to the days of David with nostalgia and longing.

During the period of history that followed the Maccabean revolt from Seleucid (Syrian) control (165-63 B.C.), the Hasmoneans built a realm of considerable size, second only to that which had prevailed under David. However, after the Roman eagle was planted on Jewish soil in 63 B.C., the hope of regaining David's territorial borders died once again.

In light of illustrations l and 2, it is little wonder that when Pilate offered his audience a choice between Jesus and Barabbas, the latter got the vote. After all, he had been a rebel (no doubt against the Romans), had committed murder in an insurrection, and fitted the Maccabean image, Mark 15:7. He wanted what every self-respecting nationalistic Jew wanted – freedom from foreign domination, and "Palestine for the Jews!"

It is significant that in 1919 the Zionist movement proposed that the Jews be given a Palestine whose borders coincided approximately with those of the old Davidic empire. One concession was made to Jordan on the east bank: the border should circle west of Amman to permit that city to remain in Jordanian territory. In light of that proposal, the following comments are relevant:

> In Genesis 15:18 God makes a covenant with Abraham in which he says, "To your descendants I give this land, from the river of Egypt to the great river, the river Euphrates." During

the powerful 18th Dynasty, Egypt controlled the region from the river of Egypt (Wadi el-Arish) to the Euphrates and designated it as a province. The Israelites knew about this. Later on, someone took the boundaries of the old province to be the extent of the promised land and so he inserted the boundary notation after "land."

But this large area was not realistic, even in David's time. The fact is that the Israelites never had a consistent understanding of the boundaries of the promised land. The boundaries kept shifting back and forth over the various periods of Israel's history. The most commonly recognized definition was "from Dan to Beer-sheba." It is exceedingly doubtful that this scribal note in Genesis 15:18 is to be taken as the absolute extent of the promised land. (Dewey M. Beegle, *Prophecy and Prediction,* p. 183)

D. The Land "forever"

In any discussion about Old Testament Israel's claim to the land of Canaan, Genesis 12:1-3 and 12:7 play a crucial role. In Genesis 12:1-3, God commands Abraham to go to the land of Canaan, and promises to give him offspring and to use him and his descendants as a vehicle for bringing blessing to the nations. Further, in Genesis 12:7, God says to Abraham, "To your descendants I will give this land." In Genesis 13:14,15, God says:

> Lift up your eyes, and look from the place where you are, northward and southward and eastward and westward; for all the land which you see I will give to you and your descendants forever.

The significant term in these verses is "forever." What does it mean, literally? Beegle writes:

> The Hebrew expression behind the translation "forever" is "ad 'olam," "until a long time." The period of time covered by the term was relative to the horizons of the speaker. In some places it is used referring back to the reign of David or the time of Moses. With respect to the future, it can apply to the length of a person's life (Deuteronomy 15:17) or to the end of an age. The covenants and promises of God in the Old Testament were clearly understood to be valid for the foreseeable future, but there was no clear concept of how long that would be. (Beegle, p. 183)

There is more. When the Assyrians carried the Northern Kingdom of Israel into exile in 721 B.C., the history of that realm came to an end. Later, in 597 and 587 B.C., the Babylonians carried off the Southern Kingdom of Judah into exile. However, some of those taken to Babylon, and many of their descendants, returned to Judah during the years following 538 B.C. – an enlightened Cyrus the Persian made that possible. Much of the pre-exilic and exilic literature stresses the fact that the Lord never really *gave* the land to His people. *He remained its owner,* Exodus 19:5; Hosea 9:3, Jeremiah 2:7; cf. also Leviticus 25:23,24. The Israelites were at best *tenants* in the land. They held it in trust from him. Furthermore, their length of stay in the land would be determined by what they did with the stipulations (law codes) of the Sinai covenant. If they took the law codes seriously and sought to obey them, they would remain in the land; if they did not, the Lord would throw them out of the land and send them into exile, Deuteronomy 4:25-31; 8:11-20; ch. 28; Leviticus 26.

When did the Jews begin consistently to stress that they had permanent title to the land, and that God would eventually bring that state of affairs about? This development took place in the postexilic era, the period after 538 B.C. One can well understand why it took place. No doubt their troubled pre-exilic history, and their experience of exile in Babylon, gave birth to a longing for a stable, assured, continuing history within the land, Amos 9:11-15; Ezekiel 34:25-31. After all, once to Babylon was enough! God would bring this about, not just to provide his people with some kind of Utopia, but to establish a setting in which they could devote themselves to being the obedient people he had always wanted them to be. God remained the God of the covenant. He had permitted the Assyrians and Babylonians to maul his people in order to bring them to their senses, Ezekiel 36:16-21. He would act again in mercy to mold them into a responsive, obedient people, Jeremiah 31:31-34; Ezekiel 36:22-32.

An important question is: Why did God act as he did over the centuries with Israel? His concern was not merely Israel's comfort or privilege. His desire was to have an obedient, servant people whose praise of his mercy and obedience to his will would serve as a magnet to attract other nations into the sphere of his redemptive grace and mercy, Genesis 12:3; Deuteronomy 4:1-8. Jeremiah lamented bitterly the fact that the Israel of his day was doing anything but taking that high calling seriously, Jeremiah 4:1,2.

There is reason to believe that during the intertestamental period, Israel lost sight of her high calling, and that she not only longed for some idyllic period of history for herself, but longed also for the destruction of those Gentile nations which had made life difficult for her; read, for example, the "doom oracles" of the prophets, such as Jeremiah 51:59-64; Ezekiel chs. 25-32; Obadiah 8-21; Joel 3; Psalm 137:7-9. In this context, it is also essential to know something about the spirit of writings such as First and Second Maccabees where the writer seemingly finds delight in reporting how the *Hasidim* slaughtered tens of thousands of their enemies, and practiced extreme brutality in doing so. Third Maccabees 7:10-16 tells how Jews in Alexandria put to death more than 300 fellow Jews who had not been sufficiently zealous in practicing Judaism. Sirach 50:25-26 consists of an invective against Judah's neighbors: the Edomites, the Philistines, and the Samaritans – the latter being referred to as "fools." All the more remarkable that Jesus saw fit to tell a parable about a Samaritan whose compassion and mercy far outstripped that shown by Temple operatives such as a priest and a Levite, Luke 10:25-37!

The term "forever" has created considerable confusion in relation to so-called divine promises concerning the Israelites as God's people, the land, Jerusalem, the Temple and the Davidic dynasty. True, passages do refer to Abraham and his descendants being given the *land* forever, Genesis 13:15; to the Israelites as being declared God's *people* forever, 2 Samuel 7:24; to *David's dynasty and kingdom* lasting forever, 2 Samuel 7:13,16,25,29; to the *Temple* being God's dwelling place forever, 1 Kings 8:13.

However, a short but very important word emerges in 1 Kings 2:4 – namely, "if." That little word shows up numerous times in the chapters that follow, 3:14, 6:12, 8:25, 9:4. It reaches its "grand finale" in 9:6-9 where the people are told that if they serve other gods and worship them, they will lose the Promised Land (which would include Jerusalem), their status as God's people, and the Temple.

In 1 Samuel 13:14, David is alluded to as "a man after God's own heart." To make sense out of the Old Testament narrative and Jesus' ministry, it is essential to understand what that term means. It means that God's people must worship their one God in one place – in Jerusalem. David brought the Ark of the Covenant to Jerusalem (2 Samuel 6) and began the practice of *worshiping one God in one place – Jerusalem*. David's death-bed appeal to Solomon (1 Kings 2:1-4) was an appeal to continue that practice – which Solomon did *not* do;

see 1 Kings 11:1-8, where 11:4,6 are the key verses. Little wonder that every northern king was dismissed as evil, in that he walked in the ways of Jeroboam, the first northern king, who arranged for his people to worship at shrines (Bethel and Dan) within the borders of his own realm rather than permit them to worship in the Jerusalem Temple – located in a "foreign" land and city, and ruled by a "foreign" king, 1 Kings 12:25-33. In all of this, one sees the seeds of ideas which took root and gave rise to the power and control exercised by the Jerusalem priesthood at the time of Jesus.

Biblical scholars suggest that there is every reason to believe that prior to the Babylonian destruction of Jerusalem in 587 B.C., ninety percent of the Israelites worshiped false gods ninety percent of the time. Joshua 24:1,2,14,15 indicate that even the patriarchs worshiped false gods in Mesopotamia and during their time in Egypt; see also Ezekiel ch. 20. Even those who fled to Egypt in 582 B.C., taking Jeremiah and his scribe Baruch with them, continued to worship false gods, Jeremiah 44:15-19. Jewish historians and archaeologists concur with this opinion.

In this context, it is interesting to read what later writings do with the "big names" of the Old Testament narrative. They clean them up and see them as virtually sinless; see Sirach chs. 44-51.

Little wonder that, in the postexilic period, the Jews (as Abraham's descendants who returned to Judah from Babylon were then called) devoted themselves with great zeal to worshiping one God (Exodus 20:2-6; Deuteronomy 5:6-10, 6:4,5) in one place, offering sacrifices *only in the Jerusalem Temple,* and to observing Sabbath, Exodus 20:8-11, Deuteronomy 5:12-15.

E. Enter – Jesus of Nazareth

Though Christians generally agree in addressing Jesus of Nazareth as Savior and Lord, not all fully understand the implications of the latter term. True, in addressing him as Lord they acknowledge him as the One to whom they owe all allegiance and obedience. However, they do not always understand the implication of the term "Lord" in relation to Jesus as an authority figure. This calls for amplification.

1. *Jesus as Lord: The Authority Figure*

The Gospel according to St. Mark repeatedly alludes to Jesus' "authority."

a. He has authority over the forces of nature, Mark 4:35-41; 6:45-52. In controlling the seas, winds and storms, he does what only the God of the Old Testament can do, Psalm 107:23-32. Therefore, he is God.

b. He is a teacher with amazing authority, Mark 1:21- 22. He does not get bogged down in a multitude of minute details, continually appealing to this or that rabbi to buttress his opinions. He says simply, "Truly, truly, *I* say unto you." He speaks with the authority of God, because he is God.

c. He declares that he has authority to reveal the secrets of the Kingdom of God, Mark 4:10,11,34. The Jews of his day believed that somehow or other they could, by their obedience, hasten the coming of the Kingdom of God. Jesus says that the Kingdom broke in *with him*. He is at once its King and its first Subject.

d. Jesus sets himself above the Law (Old Testament revelation and teaching). The Jews of his day said that the Law, the Torah, was the link between God and his people, and referred to it as the bread of life, the water of life and the light of the world. *Jesus applied those terms to himself,* John 6:35, 4:14, 9:5. In daring to set himself above the Jewish Torah, Jesus states that he is the ultimate authority, the link between heaven and earth, Mark 2:14-17,18,19; 7:1-23. The implication of these statements must have been shattering for his audience.

e. Jesus asserts authority over the Sabbath, Mark 2:27,28. He insists that what matters is the meeting of human need, not the observance of ritual.

f. Jesus demonstrates authority over the Jerusalem Temple, Mark 11:15-18. For a Jew, the Temple symbolized the presence of God among his people. However, Jesus declares that he is that Divine Presence, and the point of contact between heaven and earth, John 1:51.

g. Jesus claims authority over Satan and the realm of the demonic, Mark 3:19-27; 5:1-13. He has come to destroy the Kingdom of Satan, and establish the Kingdom of God.

h. Jesus declares that he has authority to forgive sin, Mark 2:1-12. Those who watch him in action on this occasion insist that only *God* has such authority. However, when they see the validity of his *second word* of healing, they are forced to admit that his *first word* declaring forgiveness must also have validity, and that therefore he is God.

There is more. In Jesus' day, forgiveness of sins was obtained by offering sacrifice in the Jerusalem Temple. When Jesus proclaims the forgiveness of sins to a paralytic in Capernaum (on the northwest corner of the Sea of Galilee), he breaks the link between the Temple system and the forgiveness of sins. In short, the "sin management system" is now out of the Temple, and resides in Jesus!

i. Jesus possesses authority over death, Mark 5:21-24, 35-43. He demonstrates that authority over death in others, and over death in himself.

j. Jesus dealt with the issue of "clean - unclean" as it was practiced in Judaism, Mark 5:25-34. When a woman who had suffered menstrual hemorrhaging for twelve years secretly touched Jesus in the hope of being cured – and was! – Jesus forced her to proclaim publicly that she was the one who had touched him. Though the strict ritualists in the crowd would have expected Jesus to rebuke her sternly, he merely said, "Daughter, your faith has made you well; go in peace, and be healed of your disease." In acting as he did, Jesus elevated one whom the community considered to be an outcast to the rank of "daughter."

What other authority is left for him to covet? None! Therefore, the New Testament claim that he is God must be taken seriously. If this is so, one must note next what attitude Jesus adopted to the beliefs, practices, hopes and ambitions of the world of Judaism into which his ministry plunged him.

2. Jesus as Lord: The Replacement Figure

The first twelve chapters of the Gospel according to St. John depict Jesus as replacing, one by one, a series of Judaistic practices. It is beyond the scope of this work to consider them in detail. However, these replacement episodes might be summarized as follows:

a. The Holy of Holies in the postexilic Temple was empty. The history of the Ark of the Covenant came to an end with the destruction of Jerusalem in 587 B.C., when Nebuchadnezzar totally destroyed the Jerusalem Temple. In the center of the floor area of the Holy of Holies of the postexilic Temple was a low flat stone, about 18 inches square. According to the rabbis of Jesus' day, this stone had served Jacob as a pillow during his journey to Haran, Genesis 28. In the Temple, it served as the link between God and humanity, the point of contact between heaven and earth, that place where the sins of the world were dealt with on the great Day of Atonement. In John 1:51, Jesus declares that he replaces that stone and its functions. He is now the point of contact between heaven and earth.

b. In John 2:1-11, Jesus creates an abundance of wine out of water – which in the normal course of events would have been used for purification rites. Amos 9:13 and Joel 3:18 stated that one of the marks of the presence of the Messianic Age would be an abundance of wine. Not only does Jesus' "sign" point to the presence of the Messianic Age in his Person and action, but it also states that Jesus replaces the legalistic requirements of the purification rites. He washes a person clean of sin once and for all, John 13:8.

c. In John 2:13-22, Jesus replaces the Temple itself with his own person and people.

d. In John 3, Jesus changes "admission requirements" into the people of God. The Jews of his day insisted that physical descent from Abraham automatically made one a member of God's family. Anyone else wishing to become a child of God must do so by becoming a Jew. Jesus replaces this belief with his teaching about a "replacement second birth" involving water and the Spirit.

e. In John 4, Jesus replaces traditional worship sites with his own Person. The Samaritans insisted that the only legitimate worship site was on the summit of Mt. Gerizim. The Jews insisted that the place must be Jerusalem. Jesus does away with both beliefs. What matters is not one's relation to a place, but one's relationship to Jesus' Person.

f. In John 5, Jesus demonstrates his authority over the Sabbath, and replaces the call to observe a day with the call to serve people – and so hallow every day and all of life.

g. In John 6, Jesus replaces the Jewish expectation concerning the return of the manna in the Messianic age. The manna had ceased to fall after the Israelites crossed the Jordan under Joshua, Joshua 5:10-12. However, 2 Baruch 29:8 (in the Pseudepigrapha) stated that it would fall again when the Messianic Age came. Jesus claims to be the Bread of Life, indicating that he replaces the manna expectation with himself.

h. In John chs. 7,8, Jesus replaces the Feast of Dedication, and the water and light ceremonies associated with it, with himself.

i. In John 10, Jesus declares himself to be that Good Shepherd, that Good King, of whom Ezekiel had spoken so long before, ch. 34. Many among his hearers responded with threats of violence, John 10:19-21,31,39.

j. In John 11, Jesus raises Lazarus from the dead. This sign demonstrates his power and authority over man's ultimate enemy, and the breaking in of the Messianic Age, Daniel 12:2. No wonder that this particular act (the "last straw" in John's Gospel) causes the Jewish authorities to seek the death of both Jesus and Lazarus, 11:53,57; 12:10.

It will be noted that throughout the incidents referred to in this section, Jesus is more than a *fulfillment* figure in the fundamentalistic understanding of that word. He is a *replacement* figure. What does all this imply? It implies that the New Testament Christian must think through what Jesus does with the traditional teachings and hopes of Old Israel. If Jesus is *The Authority Figure* as the New Testament insists, the New Testament Christian must note what *he* says about such things as People, Land, Jerusalem, Temple, Holy War, and Blessing in relation to Israel. He must think through how Jesus *transforms* these hopes.

F. New Testament "Transformations"

1. The people of God

Genesis 12: 1-3 outlines God's call of Abraham, and the promises made to him. Though Abraham's call involved privilege, it was above all a summons to a responsible mission. God planned to use Abraham and his descendants to sort out the world's moral chaos, the breaking in of which is described in Genesis chs. 3-11. Abraham's call was not about privilege. It was not about receiving blessings *from* the nations, but bringing blessings *to* them.

In the intertestamental period, the concept of "people of God" became increasingly equated with *the Jewish people*. The human race was thought to consist of two groups: Jews and Gentiles. Any Gentile wishing to belong to the people of God had to do so by becoming a Jew, and embracing Judaism's faith and practices.

Jesus said "No!" to that. Though he proclaimed his message first to the Jews, he rejected any notion that it was meant only for them, and that the path to God had anything to do with genes or geography. Admission into the people of God has only to do with faith in Jesus the Messiah as Savior, and allegiance to him as Lord.

Matthew depicts Jesus as establishing a true people of God. The "true" did not mean the rejection of all in the "old," for the true grew out of the old and was a continuation of God's original intentions for the old. Many from the old joined the ranks of the true. However, those who wished to belong to the true had to belong to it on the basis of the new factors. The division was no longer a matter of Jew/Gentile, but Christian/non-Christian. In short, God still has his chosen people, and a mission for that people.

2. The Land

The New Testament shows a marked disinterest in the land of Canaan as the focal point for present and future salvation history. Jesus left it on several occasions to minister to Gentiles beyond its borders, Mark 5:1-20; 7:24-30; 7:31-8:10. Remarkably, the *Gentiles* whom he ministered to in those regions seemed to know who he was, Mark 5:7. In Matthew's version of the healing of the Syro-Phoenician woman's daughter (15:21-28), the woman addressed Jesus as "Lord," and "Son of David." Furthermore, among the *Jews*, though the blind could "see" who Jesus was, those who could see were "blind" to who he was, Mark 10:46-52.

Mark contains two accounts of Jesus feeding the multitudes. After Jesus fed five thousand Jews on the west bank of the Sea of Galilee (6:30-44), there were twelve baskets of fragments left over – the message most likely being "one basket for each of the twelve tribes." After he fed four thousand Gentiles in the Decapolis (non-Jewish territory to the southeast of the Sea of Galilee), there were seven baskets of fragments left over, 8:1-9. However, Deuteronomy 7:1 (and other Old Testament passages such as Ezekiel 25-32) refer to seven nations whom the Israelites hated. Most likely the message of Jesus' actions was: God has an abundance of mercy not only for the Jews, but also for the Gentiles – those who live beyond the borders of the so-called Holy Land!

Immediately after Jesus fed the multitudes in John 6, the crowds sought to make him king of their territory. However, Jesus left them and went away by himself, John 6:14-15. The crowds were not exactly offering him any promotion, for he was already king of the universe, as the next incident clearly shows, John 6:16-21, Psalm 107:23-32. Furthermore, Jesus made it abundantly clear to his disciples that their mission was to be world-wide in scope, Matthew 29:18-20.

The ascension account in Acts is relevant here. When the disciples asked Jesus whether he was about to restore the old kingdom of Israel within the land, Jesus responded by pointing them beyond that realm, and by leaving that realm, Acts 1:6-9.

The apostle Peter has some important things to say about the location of the hoped-for inheritance, 1 Peter 1:3-5. The inheritance, which in the Old Testament was equated with the land of Canaan, is now nothing less than an imperishable, undefiled, and unfading eternal realm, which God will reveal to his people beyond death and in his own good time. In short, God still has a "land" and an "inheritance," but one transformed in location and quality.

3. *Jerusalem*

Jerusalem appears in the biblical narrative early and regularly, Genesis 14:18; Judges 1:8,21. It achieved prominence when David captured it – in a bloody and brutal manner – and made it his capital, 2 Samuel 5:6-10. Indeed, he called it "the city of David," 2 Samuel 5:9.

Statements made about Jerusalem's importance and security vary. Isaiah twice insisted that it would not fall. The first assurance that it would not fall (Isaiah 7) was given in 735 B.C. when Syria and Israel were besieging Jerusalem in an attempt to force King Ahaz to join them in a revolt against Assyria. Isaiah's second assurance (37:33-35) was given during Sennacherib's siege of Jerusalem in 701 B.C. Remarkably, Micah, *a contemporary of Isaiah*, insisted that Jerusalem would be reduced to rubble, Micah 3:12.

Exilic and postexilic writers sing its praises, and see it as the focal point of all salvation history, e.g., Isaiah 62 and numerous psalms.

The Gospels speak of Jerusalem as that city which is opposed to Jesus' person, ministry and mission. The further Jesus is away from it, the more secure he feels. The closer he moves to it, the greater his awareness of his impending death. He grieves over it, Luke 13:34,35, and predicts its destruction, Luke 13:34,35; 19:41-44. In Matthew, Mark and Luke, Jesus' ministry takes place in Galilee. He enters Jerusalem for the first time *during his ministry* on Palm Sunday, is crucified five days later, and in Matthew and Mark is seen, or will be seen, in Galilee beyond his resurrection, Matthew 28:16-20; Mark 16:7. In John's Gospel, the final scene beyond Jesus' resurrection also takes place in Galilee, ch. 21.

In his Christmas narrative (2:1-7), Luke refers to **Bethlehem** as the city of David (v. 4), and with good reason, for eventually the traditional "city of David" became the "city of death" for Jesus. Little wonder that John encourages those being persecuted for their faith in Jesus the Messiah by assuring them that they would eventually see the *eternal, heavenly* Jerusalem, Revelation 21:1-4.

In Luke's narrative, an imperial decree results in Joseph taking Mary to Bethlehem. The closing scene in Luke's Gospel refers to Jesus' ascension from the Mount of Olives, and the disciples going to the Temple to pray – not to offer sacrifice, 24:50-53. However, Luke wrote not only a Gospel but also Acts. In the closing scene in Acts ch. 28, Paul is in Rome where he is to be tried by the Emperor or his representatives. No doubt he would have taken advantage of the occasion to state: Jesus is Lord, Caesar is not. Jesus rules the world, Caesar does not. Jesus brings peace, Caesar does not. Jesus brings peace through his Word and mission; Caesar's swords bring no peace!

To sum up: Though Jerusalem as a city still has great historical significance for Christians today, their "real Jerusalem" has shifted location, Galatians 4:26.

4. Temple

In Genesis 22:1,2, Abraham is told to offer his son Isaac as a sacrifice on a mountain in the land of Moriah; 2 Chronicles 3:1 identifies that mountain as Jerusalem. 2 Samuel 24 speaks of David buying a threshing floor in Jerusalem from Araunah the Jebusite, and offering sacrifice on it. Later Solomon built his Temple on that site. Perhaps the point the writers wish to make is this: The Temple is such a holy place, for both Abraham and David offered sacrifice on the site where it was built.

Jerusalem first achieved prominence as a worship site when David brought the Ark of the Covenant, the focal point of the old Tribal League, into his new capital city, 2 Samuel 6. After this event, though Jerusalem might have been thought of as an important worship site, perhaps even *the* most important worship site, there was no suggestion that it be the *only* worship site. Most scholars agree that it became the only legitimate worship site in connection with Josiah's reform in 621 B.C.; see 2 Kings 22,23.

Though in the minds of many, Solomon's Temple was a holy and godly place, the opposite is true. Ancient Israel's prophets questioned the divine origin of the sacrificial system, Amos 5:25; Jeremiah 7:21-23. They generally attacked the system, Isaiah 1:10-20; 58:6-9. Furthermore, child sacrifice was practiced until the time of the Babylonian campaigns in 597 and 587 B.C. (2 Kings 23:10, Jeremiah 8:30-34), indicating that the religious practices of the Israelites were not what many believe them to have been.

When Josiah carried out his reform in 621 B.C. (in which he cleansed the Temple and centralized the sacrificial system in Jerusalem), he eliminated the following from within its precincts: the worship of the fertility gods; the worship of the heavenly bodies; male Temple prostitutes; women who wove hangings for the fertility gods; child sacrifice; horses and chariots dedicated to the sun; altars linked to Ahaz and Manasseh; pagan worship sites Solomon had built 300 years earlier for the worship of foreign deities such as Astarte, Chemosh and Milcom; mediums, wizards, teraphim, idols and other abominations (see 2 Kings 23:4-14,24).

The first Temple was destroyed in 587 B.C. Its postexilic replacement was dedicated in 515 B.C. Though the Temple system played a more prominent role in the postexilic period, social justice continued to be sorely lacking; the rich and the powerful continued to exploit the population at large, Nehemiah 5:1-5.

In 19 B.C., Herod the Great set about rebuilding and refurbishing the entire Temple complex. The project was completed long after his death, in about 63 A.D. The Romans destroyed the edifice in 70 A.D.

Robert G. Hammerton-Kelly provides us with a fascinating description of the Temple system that prevailed during Jesus' ministry (*The Gospel and the Sacred:* Minneapolis, Fortress Press, 1994, p. 15):

> The temple stood as a sign for the need of victims; every day, it offered public and private sacrifice for the good of society. It was the supreme religious and political institution in Judea at the time of Jesus.
>
> It overshadowed Jerusalem and dominated life in the city. Eighty percent of employment in Jerusalem depended on the temple, not only day to day on its ritual needs but also on the periodic pilgrim festivals and the ongoing building project which it constituted. Nine thousand priests and Levites worked there, although not at the same time, operating what was in fact a giant abbatoir (*slaughter house*). The twice-daily sacrifices on the vast ever-burning altar consumed thousands of animals and forests of wood. There were cattle pens on the north side and sometimes the water of the Kidron stream where the blood was flushed became so thick that it was sold to farmers as fertilizer. Over it all hung a pall of smoke from burning flesh, and when the great pilgrim festivals, like Passover, were in full swing the priests stood in blood sacrificing the victims of private offerings. Jews were expected to make the pilgrimage to the temple three times a year, twice in the spring – at Passover and Pentecost – and once in the fall, at Succoth. Therefore Jerusalem thrived on what today would be called the convention business. This combination of smoke, blood, and business, whose priests were in league with Roman power to preserve their office and their landed interests, was the historical reality of the sacred for the Gospel of Mark.

Jesus dealt rather harshly with what was going on in the Temple in his day, Mark 11:15-19. He declared that he replaced it with himself and his new community, John 2:13-22. God now dwells in and among his people, 1 Corinthians 3:16; 2 Corinthians 6:16. The "stones" of his new Temple are living people, 1 Peter 2:5. Jesus himself is the "servant" Cornerstone that gives it shape, and the apostles and prophets were the first stones gathered in. The whole edifice continues to grow in size as more come to know Jesus the Messiah in faith, and follow him in service, Ephesians 2: 9-22. In short, God still has his "Temple."

There is an intriguing link, seldom referred to, between the Old and New Testament narratives. While David was besieging Jerusalem (2 Samuel 5:6-10), the Jebusites within its walls mockingly suggested he would never capture it! Why, even if its defenders were all blind and lame, they could keep David out! But David's forces managed to get into the city, most likely by crawling through a water shaft that led into the city from the Gihon spring east of its walls. After capturing Jerusalem, David gave the order to kill all the "blind and lame" within its walls, for they were hated by David's soul. More! From that day forth, no blind or lame person was permitted to enter the Temple. However, the first thing Jesus did after cleansing the Temple was to heal the blind and the lame, Matthew 23:14.

5. *War*

The concept of "holy war" plays a prominent role in the Old Testament, but is transformed in the New Testament. The five stages that emerge are:

a. During Israel's early history (the Exodus, the conquest described in Joshua, and the period of the Judges), the conviction is that God fights for his people and gives them the victory.

b. In the time of the kings, the decision to go to war is often based on expediency and national ambition, 1 Kings 22.

c. The pre-exilic prophets insist that Holy War is still very much in vogue, only that *God has now declared war on his own people!* They have ignored and broken the covenant. They seek security in force of arms, fortresses, and foreign alliances. The Lord will come to tear them apart, as a wild beast would rend a helpless victim, Hosea 13:4-8. He will throw them out of the land, Hosea 9:6.

d. In the postexilic period a change takes place. The Lord will now fight for Israel once again, and punish those who have made life so difficult for her, Obadiah 11-18, Joel 3.

e. The New Testament speaks of a completely different kind of Holy War. The sword is to be put away altogether; use of it can only bring tragedy, Matthew 26:51-53. The Christian is now to engage in battle with the demonic; his weapons are those provided by God, Ephesians 6:10-18. The demonic is every spirit, power, pressure or institution that seeks to divert people from living to glorify God by serving others into serving themselves.

6. *Weal and Woe in Relation to Treatment given to political Israel*

The central factor in Abraham's mission was that God planned to use him and his descendants to bring blessings to the nations. Those blessings had nothing to do with being in fellowship with Abraham. They had everything to do with being in fellowship with the *God* of Abraham. Israel herself was never promised some kind of automatic blessing, just because she constituted the so-called "chosen people." Her own condition under God depended entirely on what she did with the Sinai covenant, Leviticus 26; Deuteronomy 28. Other nations would find blessing in coming to know, not Israel, but the God of Israel, Isaiah 2:24. Israel was to point to him, and him alone.

As Exodus 4:21-23 speaks of Old Israel as "the son of God," so Mark 1:1 and 15:39 speaks of Jesus as the new Son of God. Jesus is the first of the True Israel, descended from the Old Israel, Matthew 1:1-17. Matthew depicts Jesus as witnessing to all Jews, with a division emerging between Old Israel and the disciples, whom Jesus gathers to himself and molds into the True Israel. The same development takes place from John 2-12 to John 13-17.

The terms "blessing" and "curse" still stand in the New Testament. However, they speak, not to one's attitude to Old Israel, but to one's attitude to Jesus the Messiah. Those are "blessed" who know the Father's forgiving mercy in Jesus, crucified and risen, and seek unselfishly to serve Jesus through serving those in need around them. Those are "cursed" who reject the gift of forgiving mercy and the summons to serve, Matthew 25:31-46.

In short, God still has his "Israel." However, what we experience in life – whether weal or woe, blessing or curse – is determined by our relationship to the Savior and Lord of that new Israel. The crux is Jesus the Messiah.

7. The Will of God for Humanity

To ask, "How many commandments has God given us?" is to invite a variety of answers. Jewish scholars would answer as follows:

a. God gave humanity's first parents, Adam and Eve, two commandments. They were to serve God and each other.

b. After the flood of Noah (Genesis 7-9), God gave humanity seven commandments, referred to as the Noachic commandments. These were given to all people of all times.

c. One of Noah's descendants was Shem, from whom came Abraham, Isaac, Jacob, and the Israelites. Those rescued in the exodus and gathered around God at Sinai were all Israelites. The covenant God made at Sinai was made with the Israelites, and the commandments spelled out at Sinai were given to the Israelites. Though Christians traditionally see themselves linked to the "ten commandments" given at Sinai, Jewish rabbis correctly point out that those commandments were given only to the Jews. Furthermore, they point out that not merely ten, but 613 commandments were given at Sinai – plus many oral traditions which were transmitted in memorized form and written down only about 200 A.D. in the Mishnah.

How many commandments have been given to Christians? The answer is "One." Jesus refers to that commandment in John 13:1-15,34,35. When Jesus refers to a "new" commandment, he does not mean an "11th" or "614th." He means that he calls his followers to seek to copy and reflect him in all they do. Each is to live as though there are only two people on the face of Planet Earth: "me – and Jesus." Jesus is all around us in disguise, and some of his disguises are distressing to behold, Matthew 25:35,36.

Though the New Testament does repeat many commandments spelled out in the Old Testament, only those Old Testament commandments are repeated which in some way serve as a commentary on Jesus' one commandment.

Paul makes a powerful point in Galatians 3:24,25. He points out that until Jesus came, God's people were directed by the law-codes revealed at Sinai. Those law codes were their "disciplinarian" (NRSV translation). The Greek word used here is *paidagogos*, which means someone who cares for children, a "nanny." Now that Jesus the Messiah has come and carried out his mission, God's people no longer live under the law codes revealed at Sinai. They live as children of God in the community of Jesus the Messiah. It matters not whether they are Jew or Gentile, black, white, colored or whatever. Frontiers and borders are a human institution, as are also national flags. God is not interested in genes, but grace. God's people are not called to conform to a code of 613 written laws plus countless oral traditions. Their status before God is this: They have been graciously forgiven and adopted into the family of Jesus, the Servant Messiah. They have been declared his brothers and sisters, God's sons and daughters. They are to seek to live in community, reflecting the mind and manner of their Lord and Brother as they share God's creation and serve each other.

8. *The Crux of the Issue*

What are the implications of the issues discussed above for life on Planet Earth in this and every age?

In *Anti-Semitism in the New Testament* (Lanham: University Press of America, 1994, p. 37), L.C. Freudmann writes:

> [Jesus] neither established universal peace, nor did he redeem Israel.... For [the Messiah's] coming, according to prophetic promises, will usher in the redemption of Israel from exile...and herald Zion as the acknowledged religious, moral and political center of all nations.

The Anglican Catechism asks the question: "What is the mission of the Church?", and answers (drawing on Ephesians 1:9,10 and John 13:34,35):

> The mission of the Church is to restore all people to unity with God and each other, in Christ.

Which of the above will being peace to the nations, and above all, to the people living in Israel and the West Bank? The answer is painfully obvious.

Conclusion

In Luke 12:13-21, we read of a man asking Jesus to get involved in settling a family squabble over a will. Jesus refuses to get involved, and tells the man that there are a more important issues to be considered. To get his message across, Jesus tells what we today call "The Parable of the Rich Fool." The major points are these: The rich man's *land* produced the abundant crops that he must store; God owns that land and its produce. Furthermore, even the rich man's *life* is on loan from God – and that very night God will ask for the return of the loan! The rich man is about to die that night, and when he does, who will own all those things he thinks of as "his"?

Though we humans are horrendously prone to concern ourselves with accumulating what we can to ensure a continuing comfortable lifestyle, we rarely understand that we own nothing, that even life itself is lent to us, and that one day we will be required to return that life to the One who is lending it to us. And then who will own all those things we have spent life accumulating?

The only hope for the world is to grapple with the mind and meaning of Jesus, and translate it into action. His desire is that all should learn that they live on a planet they did not make or own, and use a body they did not make or own. While his desire is to welcome all into his presence in the embrace of forgiving grace, it is also that all, while waiting to experience that final embrace, might learn to live together in community, asking only, "How can I use life to glorify God by serving those around me?"

About a century ago, H.G. Wells wrote:

> Jesus was too great for his disciples. And in view of what he plainly said, is it any wonder that all who were rich and prosperous felt a horror of strange things, a swimming of their world at his teaching? Perhaps the priests and rulers and rich men understood him better than his followers. He was dragging out all the little private reservations they had made from social service into the light of a universal religious life. He was like a terrible moral huntsman, digging people out of the snug borrows in which they had lived hitherto. In the white blaze of his kingdom there was to be no property, no privilege, no pride and no precedence, no motive and reward but love. Is it any wonder that the priests realized that between this man

and themselves there was no choice, but that he or their priestcraft should perish? Is it any wonder that the Roman soldiers, confronted and amazed by something soaring over their comprehension and threatening all their disciplines, should take refuge in wild laughter, and crown him with thorns and robe him in purple and make a mock Caesar of him? For to take him seriously was to enter into a strange and alarming life, to abandon habits, to control instincts and impulses, to essay an incredible happiness. Is it any wonder that, to this day, this Galilean is too small for our small hearts?

Unless the nations learn to take Jesus seriously, the road ahead for humanity will be anything but smooth. If Christians wish to play a meaningful role in making the road ahead more smooth, they must learn that the six points listed in the opening section of this essay are invalid according to *Christian* scriptures. After all, God does not enter into *agreement* with any nation or person – meaning: God does not ask any nation or person for input into how things are to be between them. God does not solicit human opinions. God operates on the basis of *covenant*. God tells people who God is, what God has done for them, and what God expects of them. To belong to God is not to bask in privilege. It is ultimately to hear God's proclamation of forgiveness and his call to give life away in the service of others, regardless of border, flag or skin color. To heed this call it to become involved in *God's peace plan* for time and eternity.

Helps For Developing an Informed World-View

Harry Wendt

The first publication listed provides readers with a broad cover of world news. The following three organizations and publications focus in particular on the situation in the Middle East.

1. World Press Review

World Press Review is produced as a nonprofit educational service to foster the international exchange of information. It contains articles from the press *outside the United States*. It consists of 48 pages, costs $26.97 for one year, and is published monthly by:

> The Stanley Foundation
> 700 Broadway, 3rd Floor
> New York, NY 10003
> Phone: (212) 982.8880

The November 2001 issue consisted of 48 articles from around the world dealing with the attack on the World Trade Center in New York. What follows is taken from one of those articles:

> The world's leaders say that "civilization should be defended in all ways and at all prices." This underlines a crucial misunderstanding: which civilization they speak of is not defined. To the perpetrator of the crime, whoever it may be, such an act of madness would be impossible in a different, more just world, however pathetic and naive that sounds.
>
> In "the world that should be defended at any price," 30,000 children die of hunger every hour, while the most developed countries experience a period of prosperity unprecedented in the history of mankind. Three million children in Africa die every year from tropical diseases such as malaria because a US$1 vaccine is out of their reach. America and its allies spent thousands of billions of dollars during the Cold War to stop the spread of Communism. The task is now much more complex, and that main goal of foreign policy must be the opposite: to ensure aid so all parts of the world, including the poorest, can be integrated into a global economic and environmental network. [Senad Pecanin, *Dani* (independent weekly), Sarajevo, Sept. 14, 2001.]

2. Jews for Justice in the Middle East

This organization has produced two small booklets which are "essential reading" for those who wish to see the Middle East through the eyes of those Jewish people who insist that the Zionist movement is largely responsible for the present disastrous situation that prevails there. The titles are *The Origin of the Palestine-Israel Conflict* (40 pages) and *The Israeli Occupation: Background and Analyses of the Current Conflict* (20 pages). These publications draw on numerous Jewish writers – and others – to support their position. Though the publishers are prepared to make these booklets available to interested persons without cost, it is suggested that those ordering them pay $1 per copy. Write to:

> Jews for Justice in the Middle East
> P.O. Box 14561
> Berkeley, CA 94712

3. The Link

The Link is published by "Americans for Middle East Understanding" (AMEU). It is published every two months, and contains one major article. Two articles from *The Link* are included in this publication (one by British scholar Michael Prior, and the other by John Mahoney, the Executive Director of AMEU). A $40 annual subscription is requested to defray the cost of publishing and distributing *The Link* and AMEU's Public Affairs Series. AMEU also makes available helpful books and video-cassettes.

> AMEU
> 75 Riverside Drive, Room 245
> New York, NY 10015-0245
> (212) 870.2053

Among other things, AMEU publishes a 16-page pamphlet which catalogs events in the Middle East from 1948 until September 11, 2001. It includes the following:

> **July 1954:** Israeli agents firebomb American and British cultural centers in Egypt, making it look like the work of the Egyptian Muslim Brotherhood in order to sabotage U.S.-Egyptian relations.

In January 2002, AMEU launched a new web site (www.ameu.org) which features 50 of the most requested *Link* issues from the past 34 years. AMEU also distributes an insightful video entitled *DMZ, People and the Land*. The cost of the 57-minute video is $25, including shipping. Though this video was produced for Public Television, it was shown on very few of its channels.

Washington Report on Middle East Affairs (*MRMEA*; see below) points out that anything depicting Zionist actions in a negative light is rarely shown on Public Television or aired on National Public Radio. In a recent book, *Invisible Enemy: Israel, Politics, Media and American Culture* (distributed by *WRMEA* and reviewed in that publication's August/September 2001 issue), Edward Abboud lists 43 Hollywood films since 1967 that glorify heroic Israeli leaders and vilify Arabs. He also examines the influence those sympathetic to the Zionist cause have at National Public Radio, and documents that, since the late 1940s (when Israel was established), Zionism has tried to establish a collective world guilt for the Holocaust and support for Israel. In reviewing and endorsing Abboud's book, Andrew Killgore, the founder and president of the American Educational Trust (which publishes *MRMEA*; see below), writes:

> Take the example of the 60 or so misleadingly named Pro-Israel political action committees. What ordinary American would ever suspect their true purpose: to elect congressmen and senators ready to give Israel what it wants, and to defeat those who won't do so? ...[these political action committees] can and have ganged up, in secret and in violation of electoral campaign finance laws, to play tricks on the American people by electing politicians they like and defeating those they don't.

The January 1998 issue of *The Link* contains an article by Richard Curtiss, the Executive Editor of *WRMEA*, about U.S. financial aid to Israel. Among other things, Curtiss points out that the United States now makes available to Israel about ten billion dollars per year. Curtiss writes:

> I was astonished to find, after only an hour in the USAID library in Rosslyn, Virginia, that as of the end of 1995, Israel – with a population less than that of Hong Kong – had received $62.5 billion in foreign aid, almost exactly the amount received by all the countries of sub-Saharan African and of Latin America and the Caribbean combined. In mid-1986, the

combined population of the sub-Saharan countries was 568 million, and the per capita foreign aid over the preceding half-century was $43. For Latin America and the Caribbean, a population of 486 million, the foreign aid total was $50 per person. By contrast, Israel's mid-1996 population was 5.8 million. The take per Israeli for American foreign aid amounted to $10,775 by 1995.

Curtiss goes on to point out that by May 1997, the total was approximately $83 billion, or $14,346 per Israeli. He continues:

> Furthermore, Israeli insists that its annual grant be paid during the first 30 days of each fiscal year, which it then invests in U.S. treasury notes at prevailing interest rates, while the U.S. pays interest on the Treasury notes it has been forced to issue in order to come up early with all of Israel's Economic Support Funds. To illustrate, in 1991 Israel earned $86 million in U.S. Treasury note interest, while the U.S. paid about $50 to $60 million to borrow funds for the early, lump-sum payment.
>
> Apologists for Israel never tire of saying that Israel has never defaulted on repayment of a loan for the U.S. government. In fact, however, Israel has not been required to repay its U.S. government loans, some of which are extended on the understanding that repayment will not be made.

He also describes in detail how "The American-Israeli Public Affairs Committee" (AIPAC) continues to exercise considerable influence in determining U.S. Middle East policy, and spends vast sums of money in doing so. Some of AIPAC's associates declare that the reason why they are so familiar with U.S. Middle East policy is that they determine it.

In an article that first appeared on August 20, 2001 (about three weeks before the events of September 11), and was reproduced in the October 2001 issue of *WRMEA*, syndicated columnist Charley Reese wrote:

> Israel's influence in both the executive and legislative branches of our government is so pervasive that Israeli politicians openly boast about it. A few years ago when Egypt threatened not to renew the Nuclear Non-Proliferation Treaty unless Israel signed it, the Israelis told the Egyptians that if they didn't shut up about the issue, their American aid would be cut off. Now, please note: This is a foreign country telling another foreign

country that it, not the United States, has the final say over American aid. (*Editor's note: The United States provides Egypt with about two billion dollars worth of aid each year.*)

Of course, it is also embarrassing (because of our silence) that the only nuclear power in the Middle East is Israel. The only country in the Middle East that refuses to sign the Nuclear Non-Proliferation Treaty is Israel. The only country in the Middle East that refuses to allow international inspection of its nuclear facilities is Israel....

America's blind support of Israel's gross violation of human rights and international law will not only cost billions of tax dollars but eventually American lives as well.

4. *The Washington Report on Middle East Affairs*

The Washington Report on Middle East Affairs (*WRMEA*) is published monthly, usually contains about 124 pages, and costs $29 for one year. It has the largest circulation of any Middle East-related publication in North America. It covers political, cultural, economic and military issues in the Middle East and the Arab world. The magazine also focuses on the Arab-Israeli peace process and U.S. foreign policy in the Middle East. Its world-wide web site is: http://www.washington-report.org

Though subscribers may not have the time to read every word of *WRMEA*, they can read selectively and have access to information available nowhere else in the United States.

>   Washington Report on Middle East Affairs
>   P.O. Box 53062
>   Washington, D.C. 20009
>   (202) 939.6050

The publisher of *WRMEA* is Andrew Killgore, a retired U.S. ambassador. He is also the president and one of the founders of the American Educational Trust, a non-profit organization founded in 1982 by retired Foreign Service Officers to provide the American public with balanced and accurate information concerning U.S. relations with Middle Eastern states. Killgore joined the Department of State as a Foreign Service Officer and served in Frankfort, London, Beirut, Jerusalem, Amman, Baghdad, Dhaka, Tehran, Bahrain and New

Zealand. He was U.S. ambassador to the Emirate of Qatar from 1977 until he retired in 1980. He has appeared many times on national radio and television to discuss U.S. Middle East Policy and the history of the Israeli-Palestine conflict and Iranian-Arab relations.

In a recent article, Killgore wrote:

> Palestinians are being subjected to shootings and closures today because Israel is winning a war far away from Palestine: a war of words. Israel and its tireless U.S. supporters are pouring millions of dollars into a propaganda war – fought on American airwaves, TV screens and newspapers – and they are winning. Their success gives Israel free rein to continue and intensify its war on the ground in Palestine. It is essential that Americans be provided with more than the one-sided picture they now receive.
>
> Who are the combatants in this war of words? The Palestinian authority has one public relations representative, along with one understaffed office in Washington, DC that is threatened with closure every time congressional supporters of Israel circulate a letter on the hill. Israel, on the other hand, has two embassies and 11 consulates in North America that work closely with U.S. media and public officials. In addition, the Israeli government has hired two public relations firms to help win its war for American public opinion and give their new prime minister (Ariel Sharon) a gentler image. As if that isn't enough, American Jewish partisans of Israel have put up more than $8 million for a think tank called "Emet," or "Truth," to help spread the message that it is the Israelis who are under siege and not the Palestinians whose land they illegally occupy. To top it off, the (Jewish) Anti-Defamation League was recently awarded a $1 million federal grant to help fund a web site on hate crimes.

The executive editor of *WRMEA*, Richard Curtiss, is a retired Foreign Service Officer. After joining the Foreign Service in 1951, he served in Indonesia, Germany, Turkey, Lebanon, Iraq, Syria and Greece. He retired in 1980 as the Chief Inspector of the United States Information Agency. Curtiss has written a number of books about the situation in the Middle East; these are listed in *WRMEA* (as are many other books and resources). One of these books was commended by former Presidents Nixon, Ford and Carter for its balanced and informative approach to a highly politicized topic. He concentrates on the Israeli-

Palestinian peace process and the role of ethnic and religious lobbies seeking to influence U.S. Middle East policy. He has appeared on many radio and television programs to discuss the Middle East.

The publishers of WRMEA have granted Crossways International permission to reproduce sample articles of the hundreds it has published.

The Israeli Deception That Led to the Bombing of Pan American Flight 103 Over Lockerbie, Scotland.

[*The October/November issue of* WRMEA *contained an article by Richard Curtiss (pp. 22,23) that dealt with the trial of two Libyans charged with master-minding the bombing of the PanAm flight. The first part of the article dealt with the trial itself. We quote from the latter part of the article which probes reasons why the bombing took place.*]

...the current U.S.-Libyan problems were deliberately instigated by Israeli actions. Unfortunately, and this is the sinister part of it, the U.S. media observe a nearly total taboo in discussing this Israeli role, although the facts are indisputable.

For example who, besides the Libyans themselves, remembers that the first victims in the brutal and seemingly endless tit-for-tat acts of retaliation involving Libya and, later, the U.S. were the 111 passengers and crew-members killed in the crash of a Libyan commercial airliner downed on Feb. 23 1973 by Israeli guns as it descended, slightly off course during a dust storm, over Israeli-occupied Egyptian Sinai for a routine landing at Cairo International Airport? The Israelis called it a case of mistaken identity. It is not clear whether U.S. journalists ever asked why the Israeli soldiers along the Suez Canal were firing ground-to-air missiles at a civilian airliner at all, regardless of its identity. Nor why the U.S. media obstinately refuse to recognize the role of this early outrage, only four years after Qaddafi came to power, and Western indifference toward it, in the shaping of his mindset about the West in general, and the U.S. in particular.

Whether the Israeli killing of such a large number of Libyan and Egyptian civilians was or was not accidental, the next documented Israeli intervention was a deliberate and successful attempt to instigate hostilities between Libya and the United States in February 1986. It led directly to the April 1986 U.S. bombing of Libya's two major cities, Tripoli and Benghazi, in which there were some 40 Libyan casualties, including the death of Qaddafi's infant adopted daughter. (She had been orphaned when her father, a former Syrian air attache in Libya, was killed in aerial combat with Israel.) If, indeed, the two accused Libyans were responsible for the Lockerbie bombing, it clearly was direct retaliation for the U.S. attack.

The manner in which Israel's Mossad (Israel's Secret Service) tricked the U.S. into attacking Libya was described in detail by former Mossad case worker Victor Ostrovsky in *The Other Side of Deception*, the second of two revealing books he wrote after he left Israel's foreign intelligence service. The story began in February 1986, when Israel sent a team of navy commandos in miniature submarines into Tripoli to land and install a "Trojan," a six-foot-long communications device, in the top floor of a five-story apartment building. The device, only seven inches in diameter, was capable of receiving messages broadcast by Mossad's LAP (LohAma Psicologit – psychological warfare or disinformation section) on one frequency and automatically relaying the broadcasts on a different frequency used by the Libyan government.

The commandos activated the Trojan and left it in the care of a lone Mossad agent in Tripoli who had leased the apartment and who had met them at the beach in a rented van. "By the end of March, the Americans were already intercepting messages broadcast by the Trojan," Ostrovsky writes.

"Using the Trojan, the Mossad tried to make it appear that a long series of terrorist orders were being transmitted to various Libyan embassies around the world," Ostrovsky continues. As the Mossad had hoped, the transmissions were deciphered by the Americans and construed as ample proof that the Libyans were active sponsors of terrorism. What's more, the Americans pointed out, Mossad reports confirmed it.

"The French and the Spanish, though, were not buying into the new stream of information. To them it seemed suspicious, that suddenly, out of the blue, the Libyans, who had been extremely careful in the past, would start advertising their future actions... The French and the Spanish were right. The information was bogus."

Ostrovsky, who is careful in what he writes, does not blame Mossad for the bombing, only a couple of weeks after the Trojan was installed, of La Belle Discotheque in West Berlin, which cost the lives of two American soldiers and a Turkish woman. But he convincingly documents the elaborate Mossad operation built around the Trojan, which led the U.S. to blame Libya for the bombing of the Berlin nightclub frequented by U.S. soldiers. The plot was given added credibility since it took place at a time when Qaddafi had "closed" the airspace over the Gulf of Sidra to U.S. aircraft, and then suffered the loss of two Libyan aircraft trying to enforce the ban, which were shot down by carrier-based U.S. planes.

A PROMPT REACTION

The U.S. reacted promptly to the attack on the Berlin nightclub. On April 16, 1986 it sent U.S. aircraft from a base in England and from two U.S. carriers in the Mediterranean to drop more than 60 tons of bombs on Qaddafi's office and residence in the Bab al Azizia barracks, less than three blocks from the apartment containing the Trojan transmitter, and on military targets in and around the two Libyan cities. Some of the U.S. missiles and bombs went astray, inflicting damage on residential buildings, including the French Embassy in Tripoli. The planes flying from England were forced to skirt both French and Spanish airspace, and one of them, a U.S. F-111, was shot down over Tripoli, killing the two American crew members.

"Operation Trojan was one of the Mossad's greatest successes," Ostrovsky writes. "It brought about the air strike on Libya that President Reagan had promised – a strike that had three important consequences. First, it derailed a deal for the release of the American hostages in Lebanon, thus preserving the Hezbollah as the number one enemy in the eyes of the West. Second, it sent a message to the entire Arab world, telling them exactly where the United States stood regarding the Arab-Israeli conflict. Third, it boosted the Mossad's image of itself, since it was they who, by ingenious sleight of hand, had prodded the United States to do what was right...

"After the bombing, the Hezbollah broke off negotiations regarding the hostages they held in Beirut and executed three of them, including one American named Peter Kilburn. As for the French, they were rewarded for their non-participation in the attack by the release at the end of June of two French journalists held hostage in Beirut."

Ostrovsky doesn't mention, however, the other apparent direct result of the Mossad "success": the bombing of Pan Am Flight 103.

Despite the refusal by mainstream American media to revisit the well-documented facts presented above, they contain some obvious political lessons for the United States. For example, the U.S. government might decide to continue its sanctions on Libya in retaliation for the deaths of the 270 victims of the Pan Am bombing, regardless of the verdict of the Scottish judges. In that case, however, true justice would also require imposition of similar U.S. sanctions against Israel for deliberately instigating the U.S. bombing of Tripoli, in retaliation for the bombing of La Belle Discotheque, a crime which the Israelis knew from the beginning that the Libyans had not committed.

History Channel's "Cover Up: Attack on the USS Liberty" Gives Crew Chance to Tell Their Story

[*This "Special Report" by Delinda C. Hanley appeared in the October 2001 issue of* WRMEA. *Hanley is the publication's News Editor. The video referred to can be purchased from the offices of* WRMEA*; $20 plus $5 shipping. Call 1-800-708-1776.*]

After 34 years, USS *Liberty* survivors finally were given the opportunity, long denied them by the government they served, to tell their story to their countrymen – at least those with cable TV. Viewers across the nation gathered Aug. 9 to watch The History Channel's program, "Cover Up: Attack on the USS *Liberty*."

The long-anticipated show, an episode of The History Channel's popular "History Undercover" series with host Arthur Kent, originally had been scheduled to air Feb. 25. With The History Channel unforthcoming about the reason for the delay, rumors circulated that, having failed to completely block the program, Israel had demanded that additional footage defending its version of the attack be interpolated. When it finally aired, the well-documented and dramatic program explored Israel's June 8, 1967 attack, at the height of the Six-Day War, on a lightly armed U.S. ship, killing 34 American sailors and wounding 172 others. Crew members Jim Ennes, Jr., John Hrankowski, Rocky Sturman, Joe Meadors, Joe Lentini, and Lloyd Painter took turns telling their story in a precise, matter-of-fact manner, never sensationalizing the harrowing attack. Film clips from the Arab-Israeli war and previous naval maneuvers, mixed with home movies and snapshots taken by *Liberty* sailors, accompanied their narratives.

Adding to the crew members' eloquent eyewitness accounts was commentary by James Bamford, whose explosive new book, *Body of Secrets*, revealed Israeli communications recorded during the attack (see Andrew Killgore's book review, Aug./Sept. 2001.*Washington Report*, p, 103).

On the day of the attack, the *Liberty* was in international waters, 13 miles off the coast of the Sinai Peninsula, listening in on the developing Arab-Israeli war – which, the show commented, both sides claimed the other started – collecting intelligence. Fearing the slow-moving *Liberty* might be exposed and vulnerable with only four 50-caliber machine guns to protect it, the Pentagon sent three messages to the ship to withdraw farther off the coast. Twice messages were misdirected to the Philippines. The ship was definitely in the wrong place at the wrong time.

In nine hours of close surveillance Israeli pilots had circled the ship 13 times on eight different occasions. They could easily see the American flag and its clear markings. Former Chairman of the Joint Chiefs of Staff Admiral Thomas H. Moorer, who spoke at a July 23 book-signing for Bamford's *Body of Secrets* held at the Army Navy Club in Washington, DC, was outspoken and skeptical of Israeli claims that pilots thought the ship was an Egyptian vessel. Admiral Moorer described the *Liberty* as "the ugliest, strangest looking ship in the U.S. Navy. As a communications intelligence ship, it was sprouting every kind of antenna. It looked like a lobster," he noted. "Israel knew perfectly well that the ship was American."

Some of the planes circled so close that American sailors sunning themselves on their ship's deck waved to the Israeli pilots. Then, at 2 p.m. on June 8, 1967, a clear day, three unmarked Mirage fighters attacked the USS *Liberty* for five minutes. A National Security Agency (NSA) surveillance plane overheard the attack. Radio operators in nearby Lebanon also intercepted Israel Defense Force orders to attack the ship, as well as the pilot's reply that it was an American ship and he could see an American flag. The order was repeated: "Attack the ship."

Then-U.S. Ambassador to Lebanon Dwight Porter was shown a transcription of the radio exchange and later told his story to syndicated columnists Rowland Evans and Robert Novak. Two Israelis actually involved in the attacks also have confirmed that Israel knew it was attacking an American vessel.

A few minutes after the initial assault, three unmarked Super-Mystere jets attacked the *Liberty* with napalm and dozens of rockets. The engagement lasted 25 minutes – 23 minutes longer than a simple case of friendly fire – killing nine men and wounding 172. When the American flag was shot up it was replaced by an extra large flag usually flown during holidays.

The survivors continued to tell their dramatic story of heroic sailors on deck who were chased and mowed down by machine gunfire, rockets and napalm. (Clean-up crews later saw shell casings that read "Fort Dix, New Jersey.") They described others working frantically below decks to destroy classified materials. Throughout the attacks *Liberty* communications experts tried to contact the Sixth Fleet by radio or teletype, but the Israeli planes jammed their transmissions and shot up their antennas.

Finally, in the few seconds it took for an Israeli plane to launch a rocket – when it was unable simultaneously to cause radio interference – a distress signal slipped through to the chief of naval operations saying that the *Liberty* was under attack from unidentified assailants and asking for immediate assistance.

The message was received and acknowledged by the carrier *Saratoga*, and Captain Joe Tulley dispatched fighter jets to come to the *Liberty's* rescue. Israel must have heard these messages and known that it had little time left to complete its mission.

In Washington, President Lyndon Johnson convened a crisis meeting to discuss the attack. With the identity of the attackers still in doubt, according to The History Channel, Johnson and his advisers, including Secretary of Defense Robert McNamara and Secretary of State Dean Rusk, decided not to risk a possible Cold War confrontation. McNamara got on the radio and said, "'Tell Sixth Fleet to get those aircraft back immediately."

When McNamara's orders were questioned, the President himself got on the radio to recall the planes. The History Channel program implied that Israel was unaware that the White House was calling back the assistance promised and, indeed sent, by the Sixth Fleet. Perhaps the Jewish state could not imagine a scenario whereby a government would abandon its own forces.

At 3:15 p.m., three torpedo boats – which finally were marked with the Star of David, identifying the ship's attacker as Israel, attacked the USS *Liberty* from the starboard side, launching armor-piercing bullets and even machine-gunning lifeboat rafts dropped into the water in case the crew was forced to abandon ship. That attack lasted 40 minutes.

Even after a torpedo blew a 30- by 40-foot hole in the ship's communications room, the *Liberty* stayed afloat. Finally Israeli troop helicopters approached, and *Liberty* Capt. William McGonagle warned his crew that their ship could soon be boarded.

There was no doubt in anyone's mind that armed troops were coming to finish the crewmen off, survivors told The History Channel. The men are convinced that because Israel believed rescuers were on their way, they did not come aboard and kill survivors. Israeli attackers finally left the crippled ship alone. The action had already moved to Washington, where, as soon as the crippled ship sent a message saying they had been attacked by Israel, Israeli diplomats were busy apologizing for their "tragic mistake." The *Liberty* repaired its engines and radio equipment and began to limp to Malta, pausing only to attach a net to close up the torpedo hole and prevent their buddies who were killed in the torpedo attack from washing out to sea.

What hurts survivors even more than the loss of their friends and boat is their own government's subsequent cover-up of Israel's attack. John Hrankowski related how, when they arrived in Malta, the crew was divided into small groups and debriefed. Admiral Isaac Kidd told crew members not to talk to their shipmates or anyone else about the incident. This is classified stuff, he told the men: "You are never, repeat, never to discuss this with anyone, not even your wives. If you do you will be court-martialed and will end your lives in prison – or worse."

No one was interested in carrying out an in-depth investigation of anything but the communications problems the ship encountered during the Israeli attack. All evidence on the ship – including 820 rocket and cannon holes – was patched up and painted over, and crew members were sent home or reassigned (and split up) as if nothing had occurred. After a long wait, Israel paid $3.5 million in financial compensation to the families of the dead and $3.5 million to the wounded, some of whom refused to accept the money. In 1982 – after Sen. Adlai Stevenson (D-IL) threatened to hold an inquiry – Israel suddenly offered $6 million for damage to the ship and "to close the book on the USS *Liberty* affair." This effectively blocked Senator Stevenson's hopes for an investigation, and the attack quickly became an official non-issue. As far as Congress and the White House were concerned, it was over.

But it wasn't over for the survivors, however. In the years since the attack, many suffered post-traumatic stress, emotional problems, nightmares, alcoholism or divorce. Others tried to escape their pain by burying the memories so deeply they wouldn't hurt. It wasn't until Jim Ennes published *Assault on the Liberty* in 1980 that the crew began to go public with their story to tell their country what had really happened to their shipmates.

Israel, in the meantime, had published four reports that contradicted many of the facts the sailors knew to be true. It claimed to have fired on the *Liberty* as a result of mistaken identity, saying its pilots believed the ship to be the Egyptian horse-carrier ship *al-Quisair* that had been docked in Alexandria for years. Israel also claimed that, once its attackers realized their mistake, they tried to help the crippled ship and its crew. "That's the purest baloney," Ennes responded in The History Channel film.

Toward the end of the program – presumably an addition made during the five-month interval between the initial and actual airings – Israeli Embassy spokesman Mark Regev unconvincingly denied a cover-up and claimed that Israel has been most forthcoming. "It was a tragic mistake that happened," Israel's Minister of Foreign Affairs Anna Eban agreed, while UCLA Prof. Stephen Spiegel explains that in the fog of war honest mistakes can happen.

On the other hand, Prof. Richard Dekmeijan said the attack wasn't a mistake and that he believes the crewmen. He told viewers that trying to minimize or ignore the assault is a disastrous error. Dekmeijan theorized that Israel had decided to capture the Golan Heights despite a U.N. cease-fire and simply didn't want Americans to learn its plans. Nor did Israeli soldiers want an audience as they massacred Egyptian prisoners of war, who were told to dig their own graves, then shot at el-Arish. Did Israel attempt to destroy the *Liberty* and its radio transcripts containing evidence of war crimes? Did it hope to sink the *Liberty* and blame Egypt?

The crew avoids trying to guess the reason Israel attempted to sink their ship, surviving crew members Donald Pageler and John Hranskowski told the *Washington Report* during a recent visit. Said Pageler, "Only Israel knows why they did it and they will never own up to it."

The questions *Liberty* survivors want answered are directed at their own government. When did the U.S. first learn of the attack? Why did Johnson and McNamara abandon American sailors? Why did they abort the rescue mission that would have prevented the torpedo-boat attack that alone claimed 25 lives?

At his recent book-signing, Bamford asked the audience why Israeli interests were placed before American lives. The *Liberty* cover-up, he warned, demonstrated to Israel that, if Washington was willing to ignore an attack on an American ship, the U.S. would wink at almost any Israeli action in the future. The *Body of Secrets* author also told a chilling anecdote about the early days of U.S. peacekeeping forces in the Sinai. The American deputy chief of mission in Tel Aviv got an urgent call from a furious then-Defense Minister Moshe Dayan, complaining that an American U-2 had drifted three kilometers into Israeli territory. "'If one of them drifts over again," Dayan yelled at his American "ally", "we'll shoot it down."

Still-Unanswered Questions

Why was *Liberty* Captain McGonagle's Medal of Honor, earned for remaining on deck and commanding his men despite serious wounds, presented in a quiet ceremony in a back room of Washington Navy Yard instead of by the president at the White House, as has been the case with every other Medal of Honor recipient? Why has no president ever met with any *Liberty* survivors?

Why did an Arlington cemetery headstone marking the grave of six missing *Liberty* comrades for years read "Killed in the Mediterranean," without even mentioning the name of the ship or the Israeli attack? According to survivors Pageler and Hrankowski, the *Liberty* is one of the most decorated ships in American naval history, with its crew members having received 830 awards. Does the Navy typically award this many medals to victims of "friendly fire"? Why did *Liberty* survivors' DD2-14 discharge documents read RVN (Republic of Viet Nam) as the area where the men served?

When Israel jammed the *Liberty* distress calls, how did they know what frequencies the ship used? Why did the U.S. government allow Israel to lie about the attack? Why won't the NSA release transcripts of their recordings of the Israeli attacks? Why has Congress, which has investigated every other incident of this kind, never conducted an investigation into the attack on the USS *Liberty*? Is it waiting until there are no eyewitnesses left alive to tell their story?

The more Americans learn about the *Liberty* and add their voices to those of the survivors, the more likely it is that Congress will act on requests for a comprehensive investigation into the cover-up.

The History Channel – and producers Tom Seligson, Andrew Rothstein and David Siegel, along with narrator Arthur Kent – is to be praised for producing (and finally airing) a thorough and thought-provoking show in which survivors of Israel's attack on the *Liberty* finally were given the opportunity to speak for their dead and wounded comrades. The patriotism and quiet dignity with which these men shared their story is a testimony to their honor and courage, and also, unfortunately, to their own government's disgraceful treatment of servicemen who laid their lives on the line for America. USS *Liberty* survivor Dr. Richard Kiepfer recently declared, "Never before in the history of the United States Navy has a Navy Board of Inquiry ignored the testimony of American military eye-witnesses and taken on faith the word of their attackers."

It's time for Washington to tell the truth.

The above articles are included in this publication to encourage readers to make use of the resources listed to learn "the truth." Those interested in knowing and acting on the truth might give thought to making use of the following suggested letter.

A Letter to the President(s) of The United States

The President of the United States of America
The White House
Washington, D.C.

Dear Mr. President,

I wish to assure you of my prayers for you. You face daunting challenges. I am encouraged that you look to God for guidance, and seek advice and support from those who share your faith.

Without doubt the events of September 11, 2001 were horrendous and something has to be done to eradicate terrorism from the face of the planet. But more is required. I believe that at this point in time you have an opportunity to prove yourself to be the greatest president in the history of the United States.

I respectfully suggest that you invite all world leaders to a meeting in Washington, and that you preside over that meeting. I suggest that before the meeting begins, everyone present should share a meal together and then wash each other's feet. Doing this will declare two things. *Eating together:* To eat together, according to Middle East and other cultures, is to declare: "We are family. We put behind us the unpleasant memories of our respective pasts. We commit ourselves to working together that all might live in peace." *Foot washing:* "We must devote life and earth's resources to serving each other in community."

The God to whom you and I look for forgiveness and guidance has no national favorites, and is not interested in flags, borders and skin colors. We humans live on a planet we did not make and do not own, and use bodies we did not make and do not own. God teaches us that there are only two people on the face of planet earth: Jesus and me. Everyone else but me is the Jesus I am called to serve, and he is all too often in "distressing disguise" – to use a term from Mother Theresa. Each of us is to devote life to serving Jesus, the Lord of time and eternity, by full time service to those around us.

This, Mr. President, is the only peace plan that will work. The cost of implementing it will be high. The cost of not implementing it will be immeasurably higher.

I pray that history will have cause to remember you as America's greatest President.

(*Your signature*)

Epilogue

RESURRECTION
(Ode on a Burning Tank: The Holy Lands, 1973)
Kenneth E. Bailey

I am a voice,
    the voice of spilt blood
        crying from the land.

The life is in the blood
    and for years my life flowed in the veins of a young man.
        My voice was heard through his voice,
        and my life was his life.

Then our volcano erupted
and for a number of numbing days
    all human voices were silenced
        amid the roar of heavy guns,
        the harsh clank of tank tracks,
        the bone-jarring shudder of sonic booms,
            as gladiators with million-dollar swords
            killed each other high in the sky.

Then suddenly – suddenly
    there was a swish of a rocket launcher –
    a dirty yellow flash –
    all hell roared.
The clanking of the great tracks stopped.
    My young man staggered screaming from the inferno,
    his body twitched and flopped in the sand.

And I was spilt into the earth –
    into the holy earth
        of the Holy Land.

The battle moved on.
    The wounded vehicles burned,
        scorched,
            and cooled.

The "meat wagons" carried the bodies away as
    the chill of the desert night
        settled on ridge and dune,
And I stiffened in the blackened sand.

And then – and then
As the timeless silence
    of the now-scarred desert returned
there – more congealed in the land,
    in the land of prophet, priest and king –
I heard a voice –
    a voice from deep in the land,
    a voice from an ageless age,
    a voice from other blood
        once shed violently in the land.

The voice told me this ancient story;
precious blood intoned this ancient tale.

"A certain man had two sons.
One was rich and the other was poor.
    The rich son had no children
    While the poor man was blessed with many sons
        and many daughters.

In time the father fell ill.
    He was sure he would not live through the week
    So on Saturday he called his sons to his side
        and gave each of them half of the land of their inheritance.
    Then he died.

Before sundown the sons buried their father with respect
    as custom requires.

That night the rich son could not sleep.
    He said to himself,
    "What my father did was *not just*.
    I am rich, my brother is poor.
    I have bread enough and to spare,
        while my brother's children eat one day
        and trust God for the next.

I must move to the landmark which our father has set in
the middle of the land

so that my brother will have the greater share.
> Ah – but he must not see me.
> If he sees me, he will be shamed.
> I must rise early in the morning before it is dawn and move the landmark!"

With this, he fell asleep,
> and his sleep was secure and peaceful.

Meanwhile the poor brother could not sleep.
> As he lay restless on his bed he said to himself,
> "What my father did was *not just*.
> Here I am surrounded by the joy of many sons
>> and many daughters.
> while my brother daily faces the shame
>> of having no sons to carry on his name
>>> and no daughters to comfort him in his old age.
> He should have the land of our fathers.
>> Perhaps this will in part compensate him
>> for his indescribable poverty.
> Ah – but if I give it to him he will be shamed.
> I must awake early in the morning before it is dawn
>> and move the landmark which our father has set!"

With this he went to sleep
> and his sleep was secure and peaceful.

On the first day of the week –
> very early in the morning,
> a long time before it was day,
the two brothers met at the ancient landmark.
> They fell with tears into each others arms.
>> And on that spot was built the city of Jerusalem.